If The Shoe Fits...

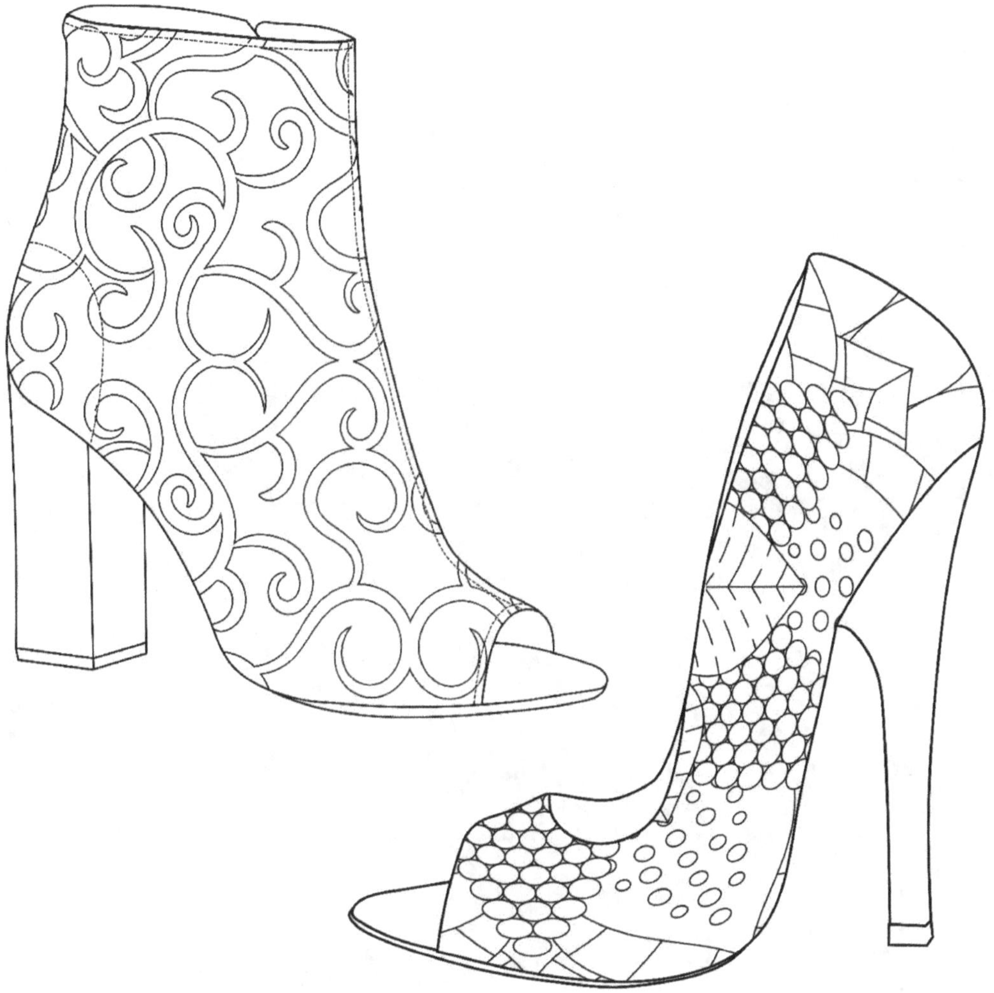

Color It!

A Coloring Book For Shoe Lovers

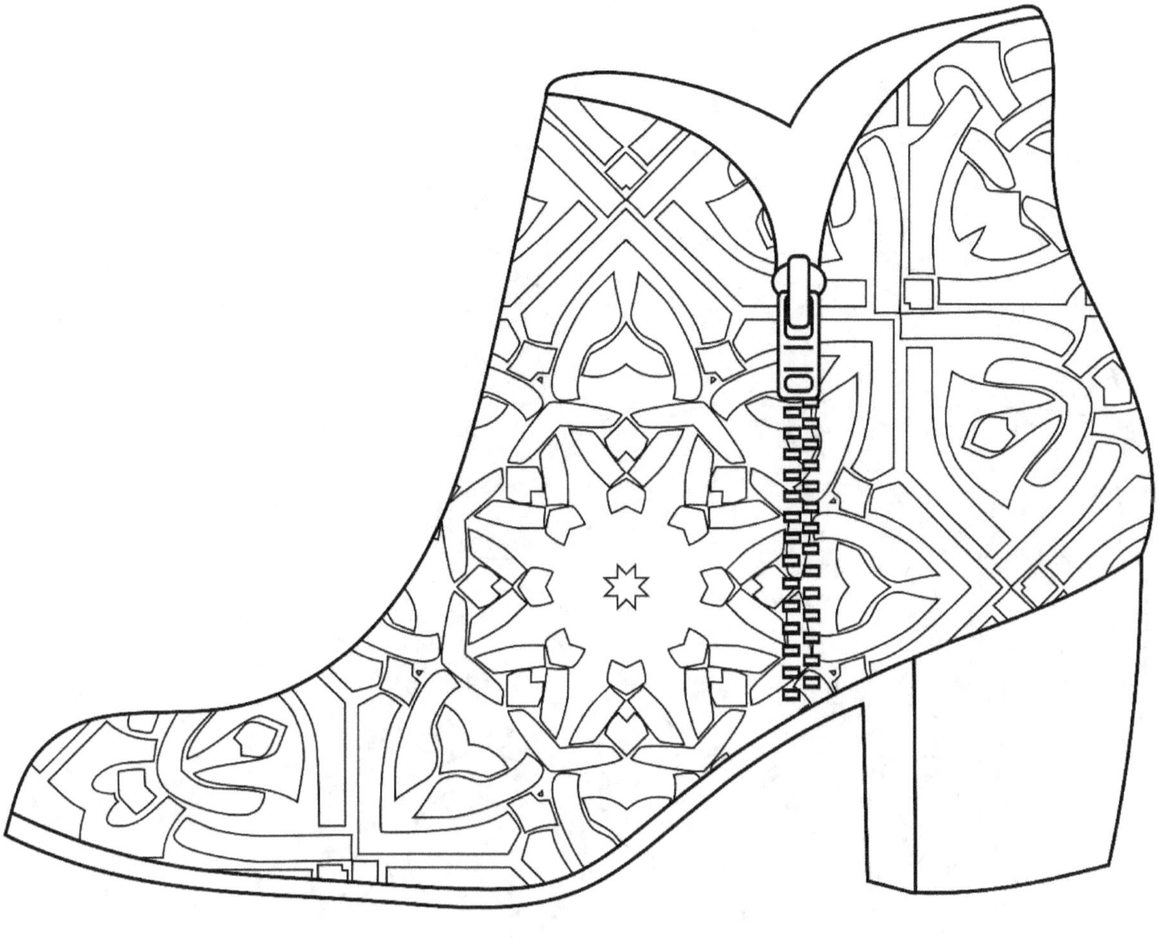

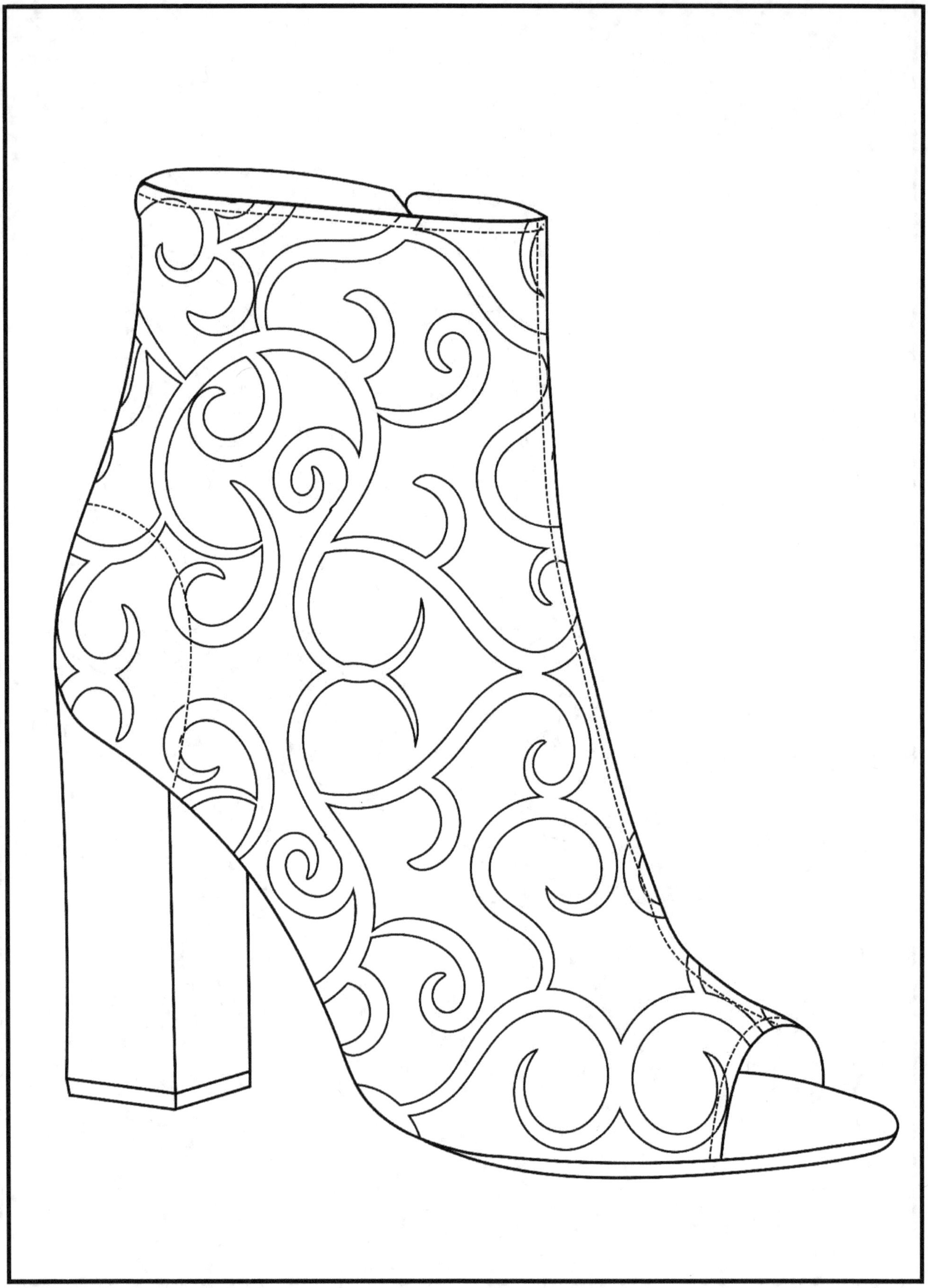

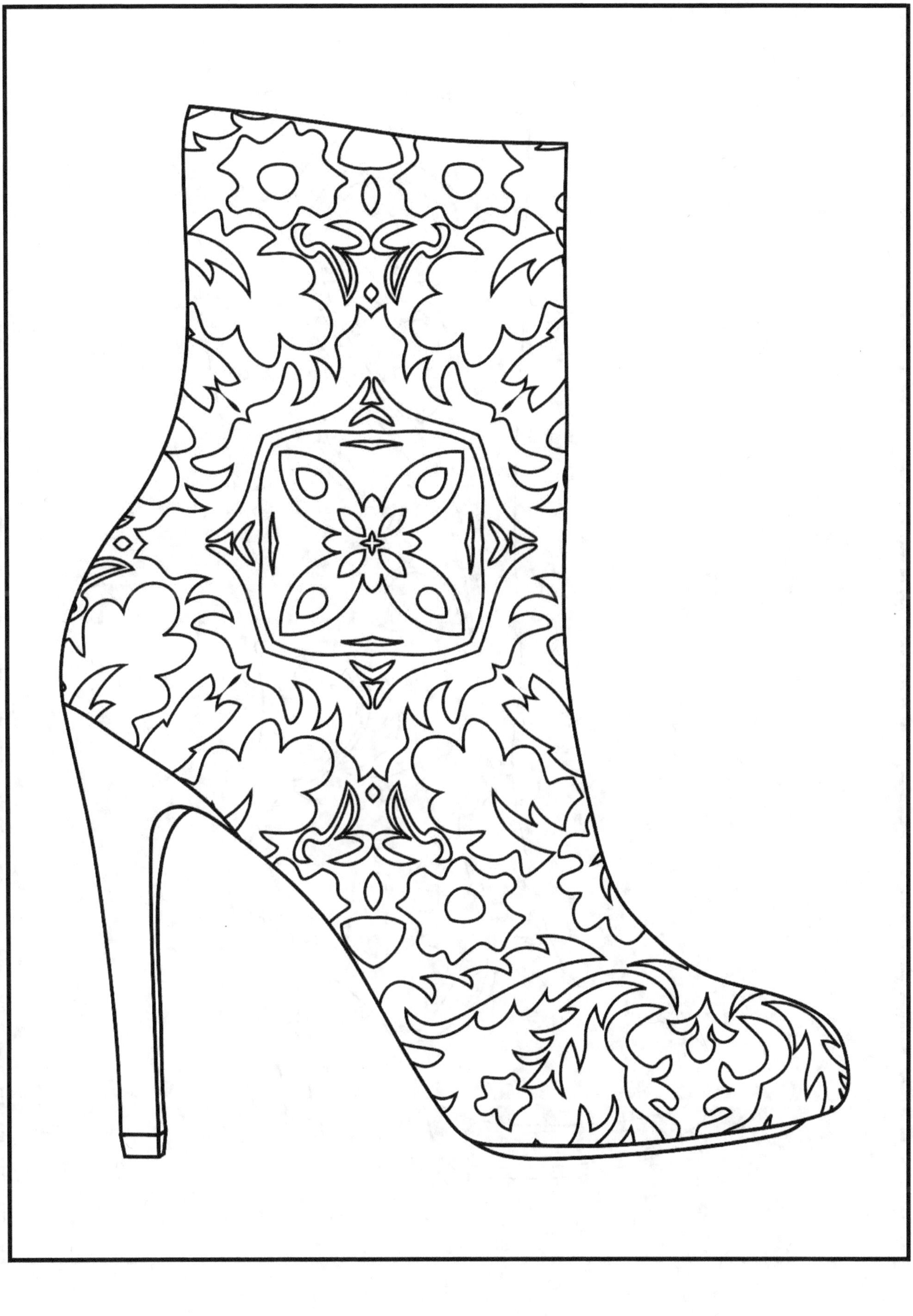

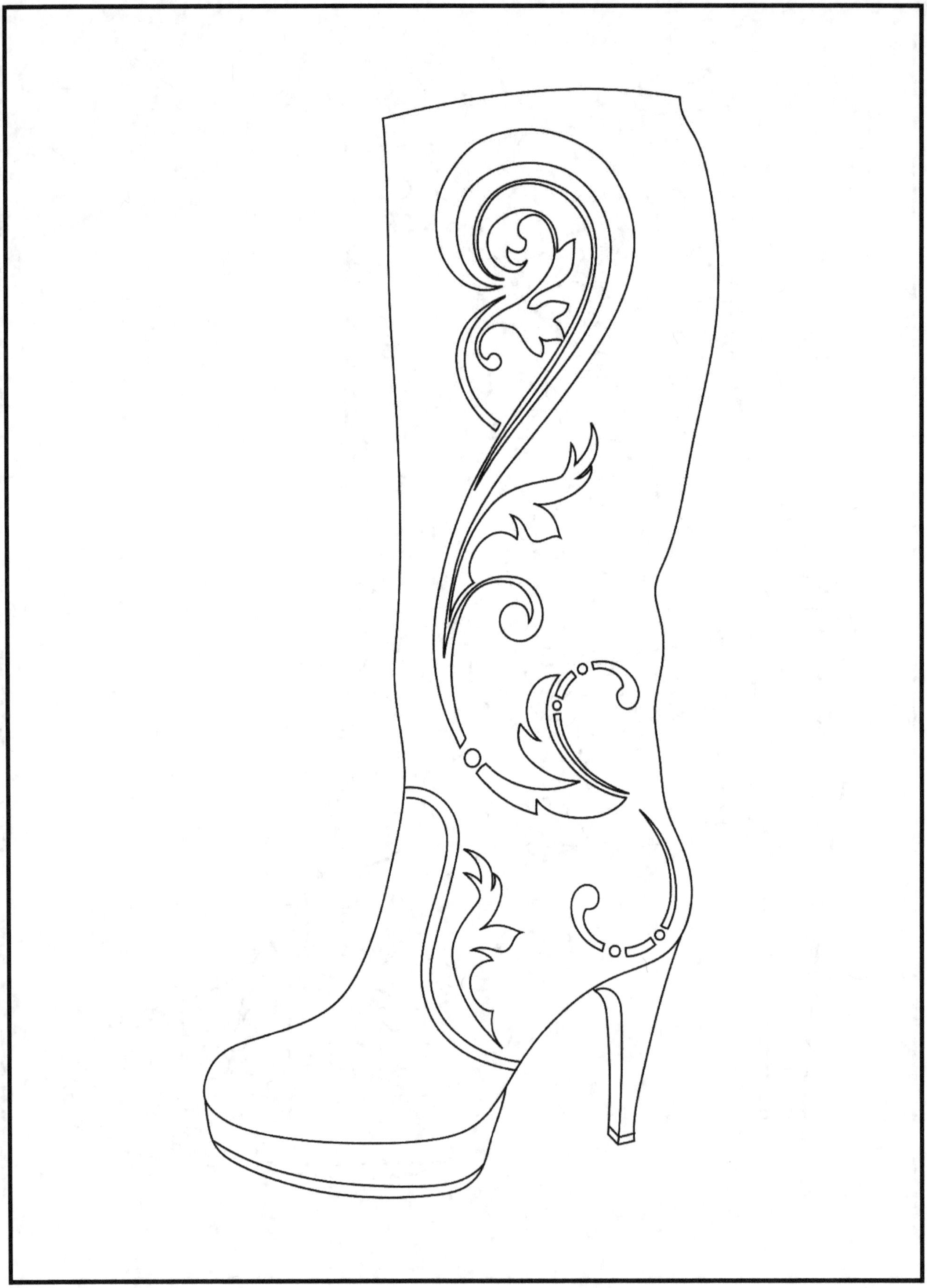

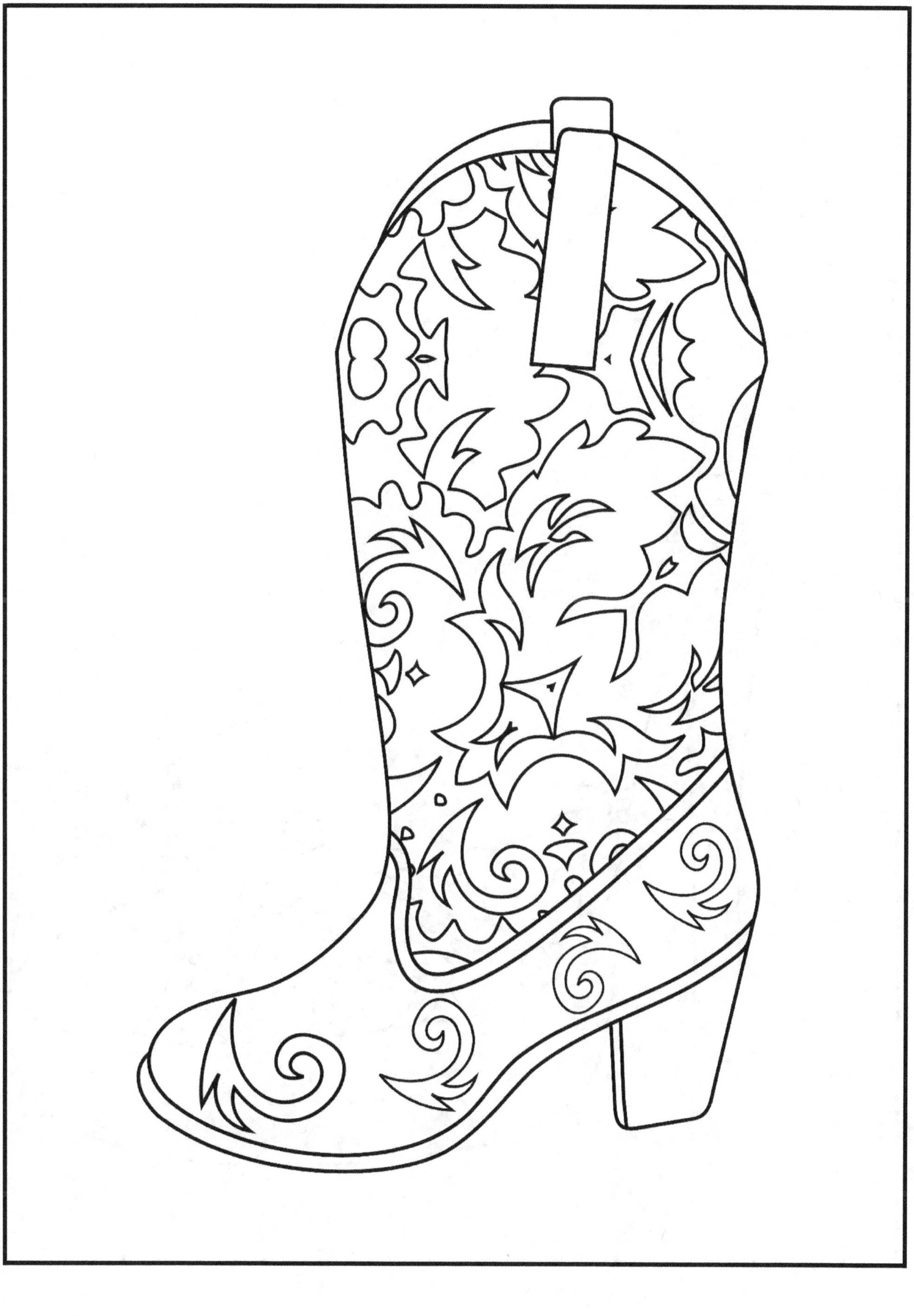

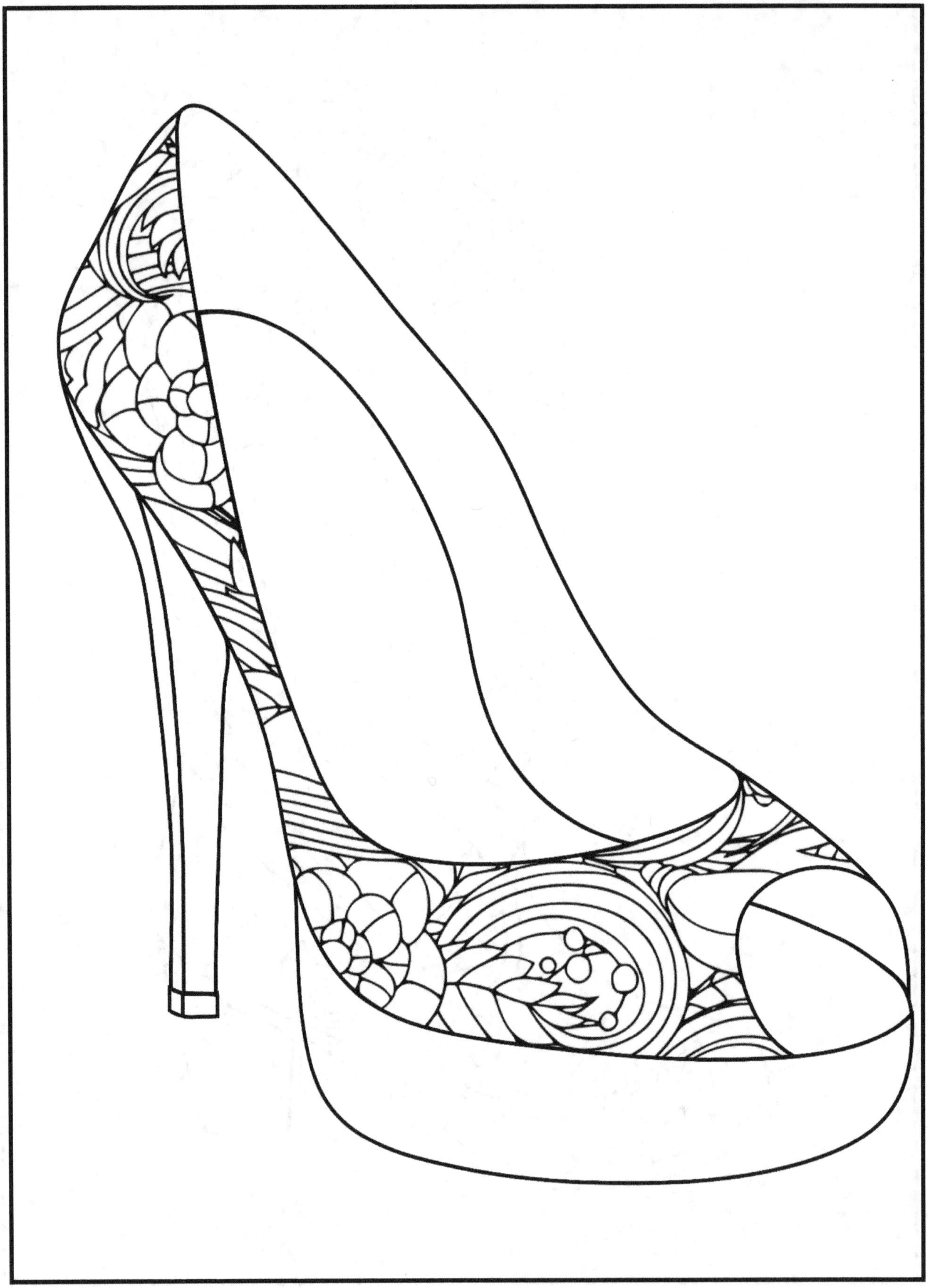

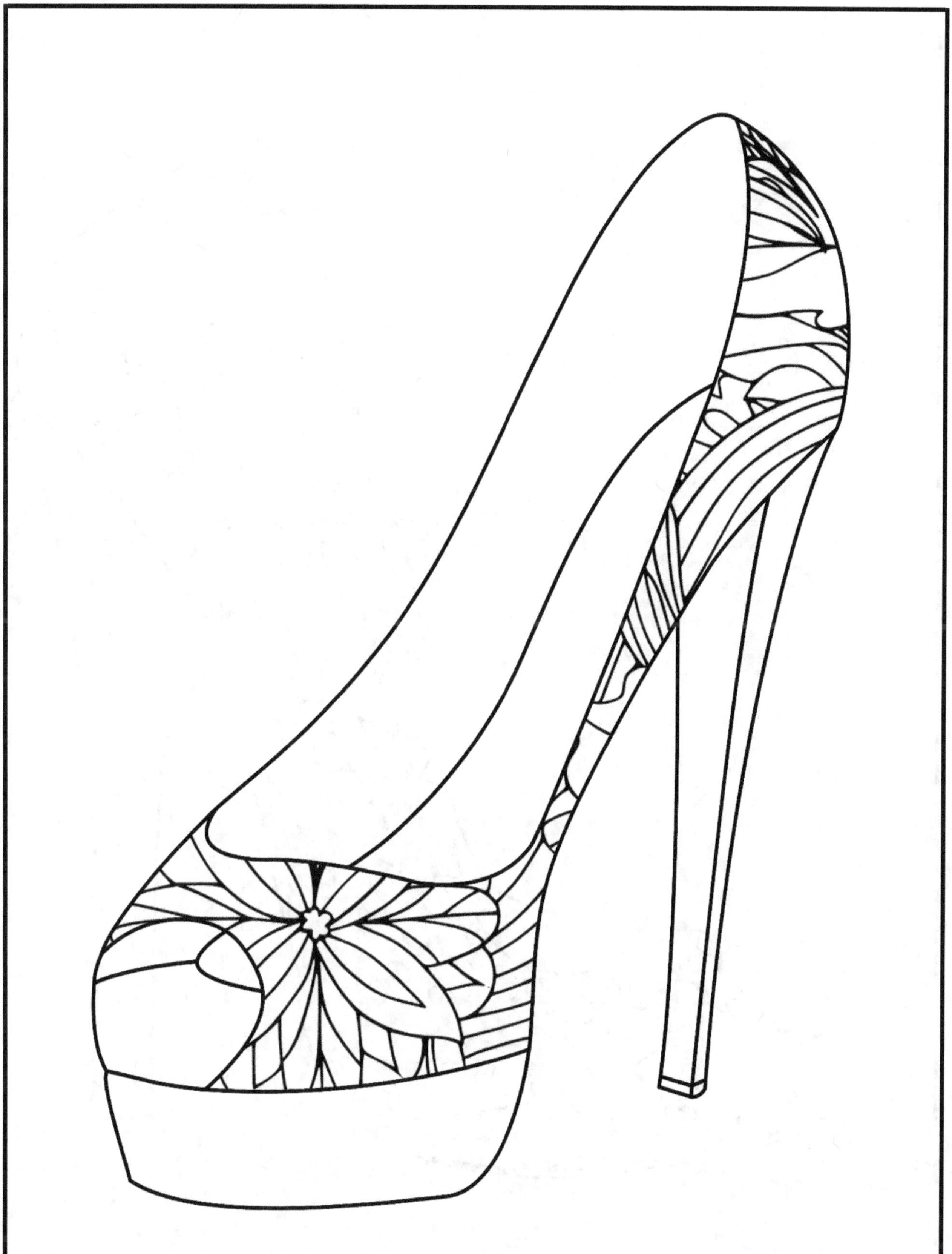

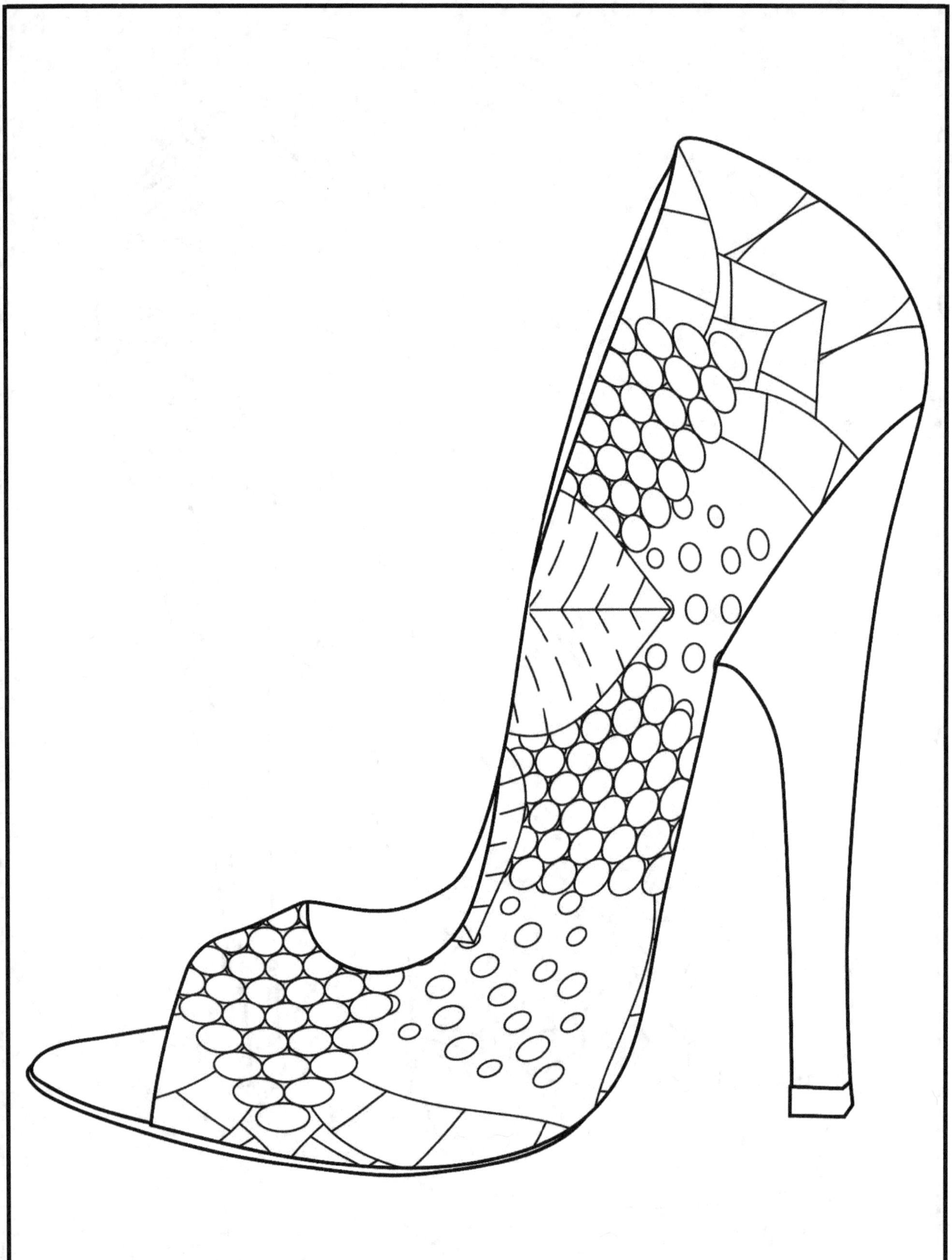

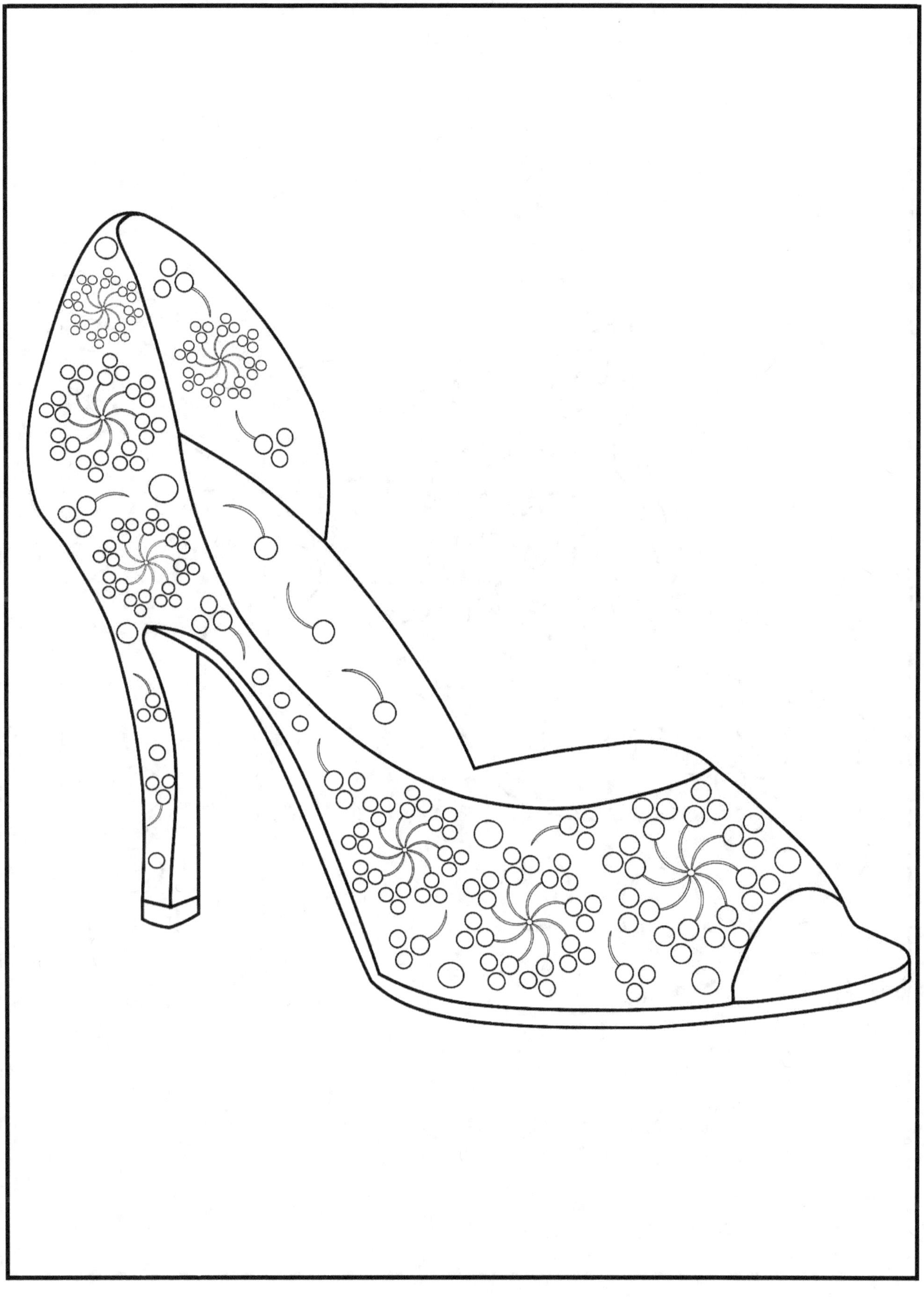

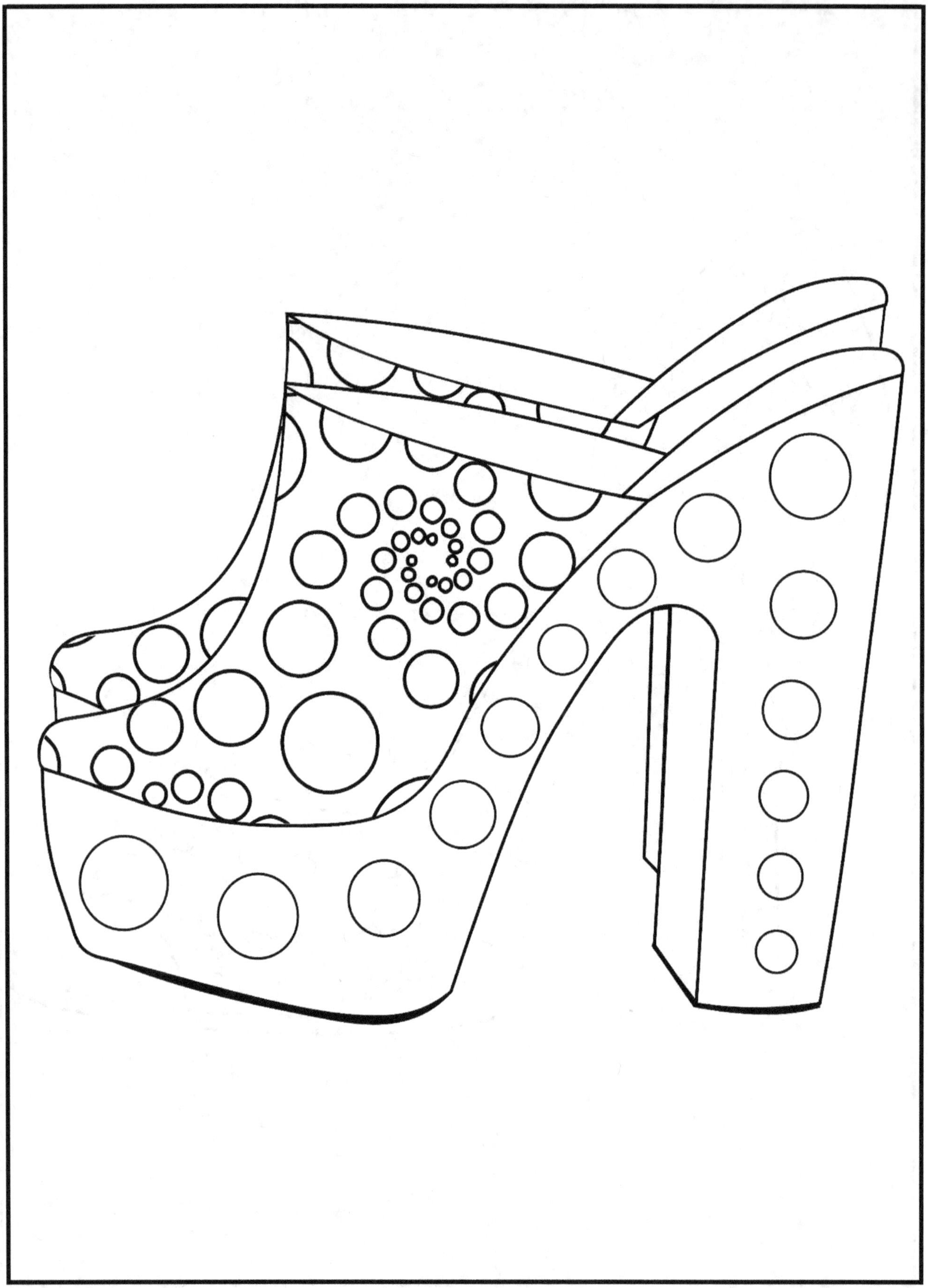

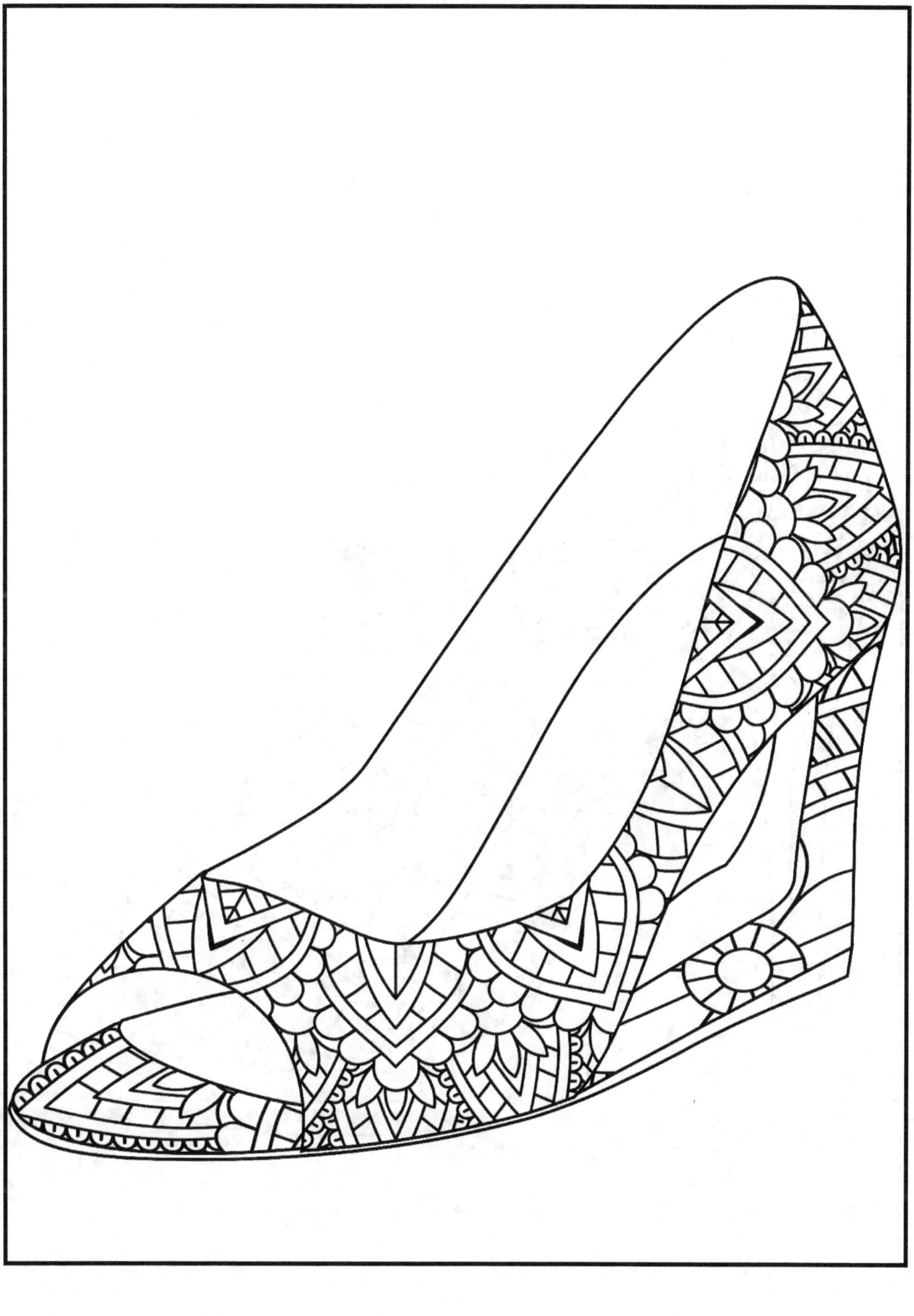

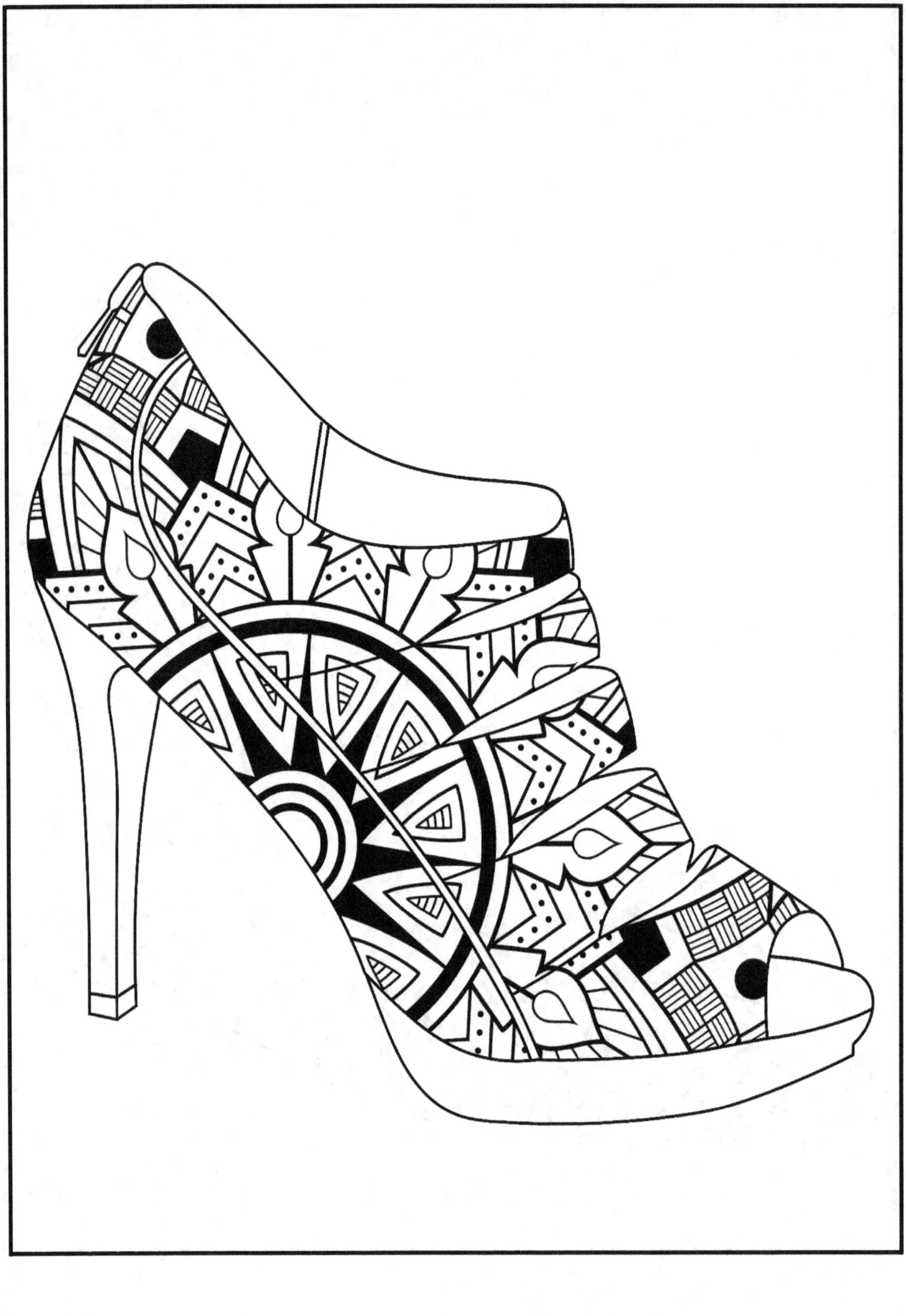

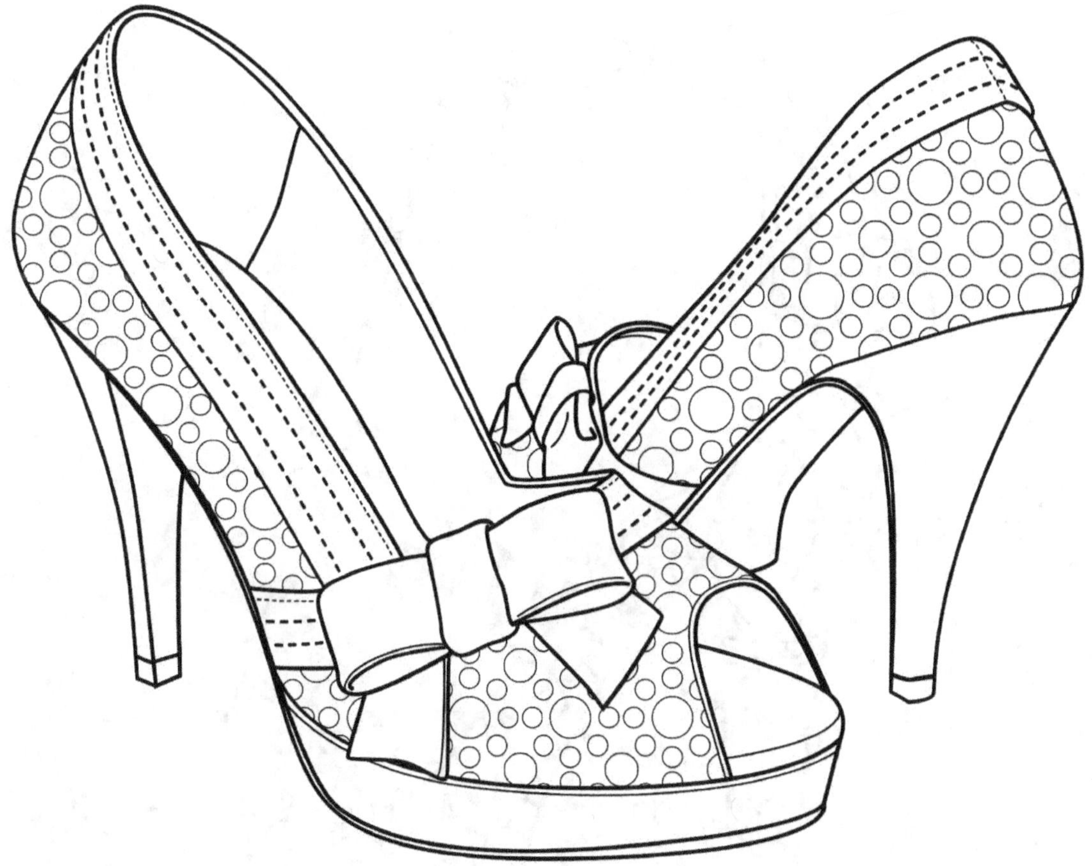

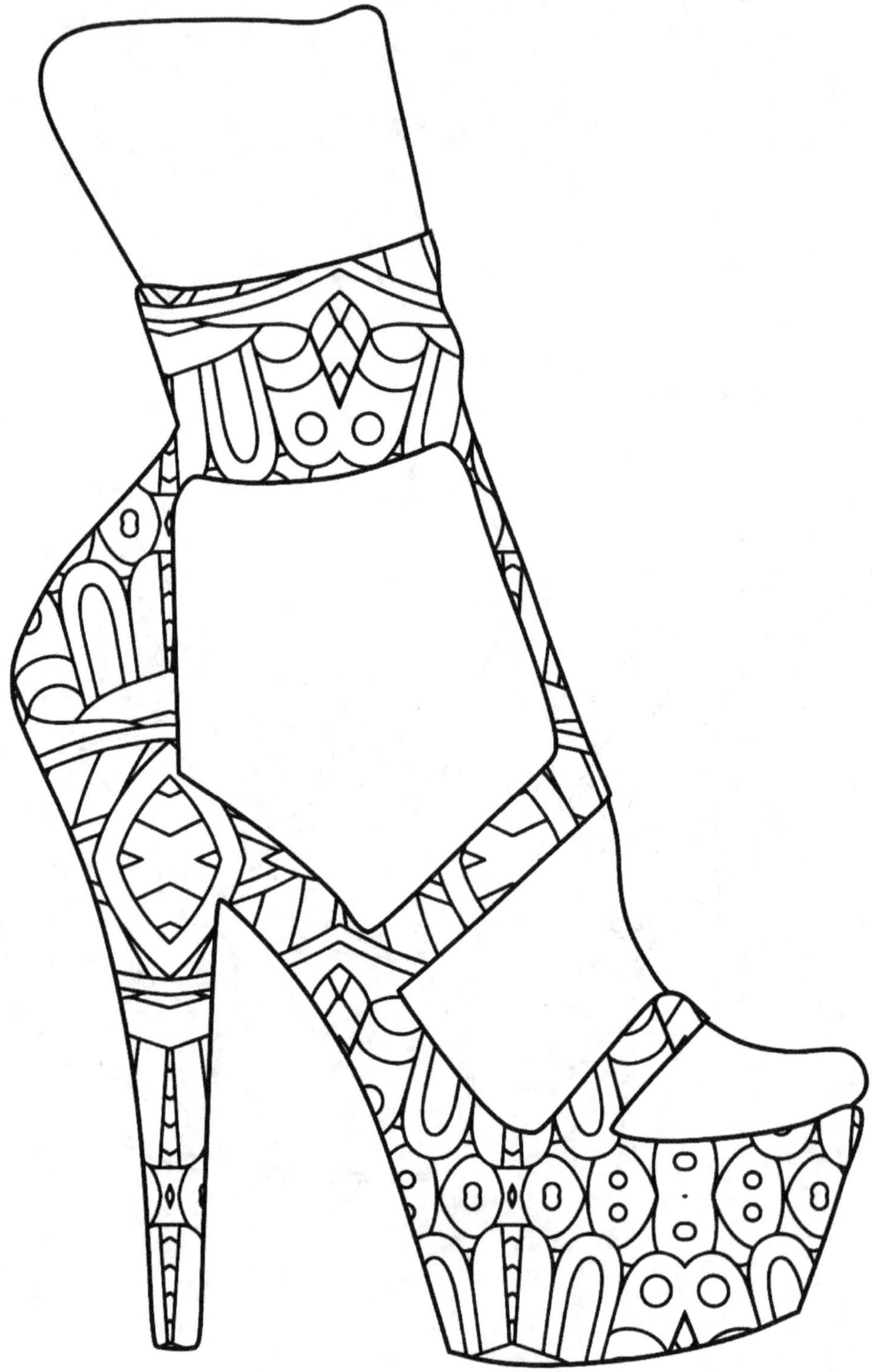

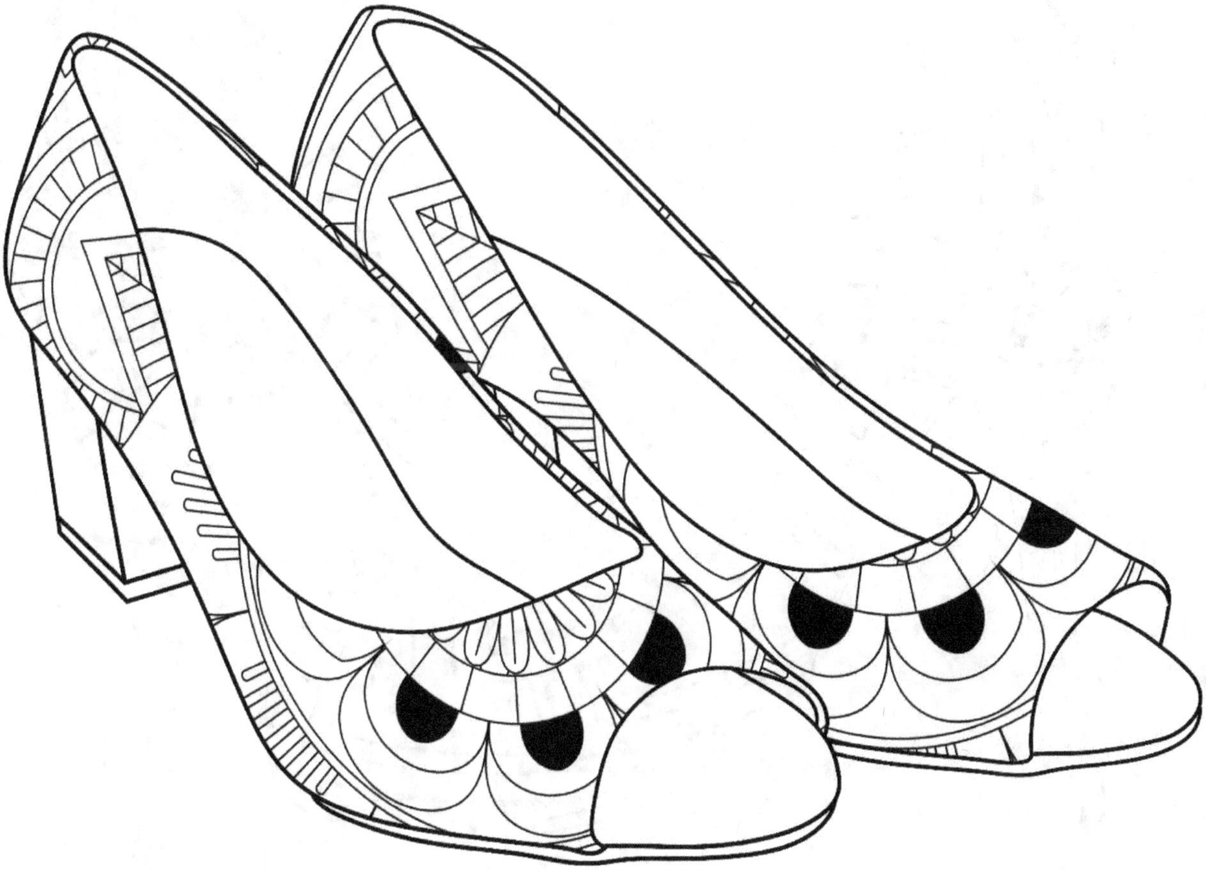

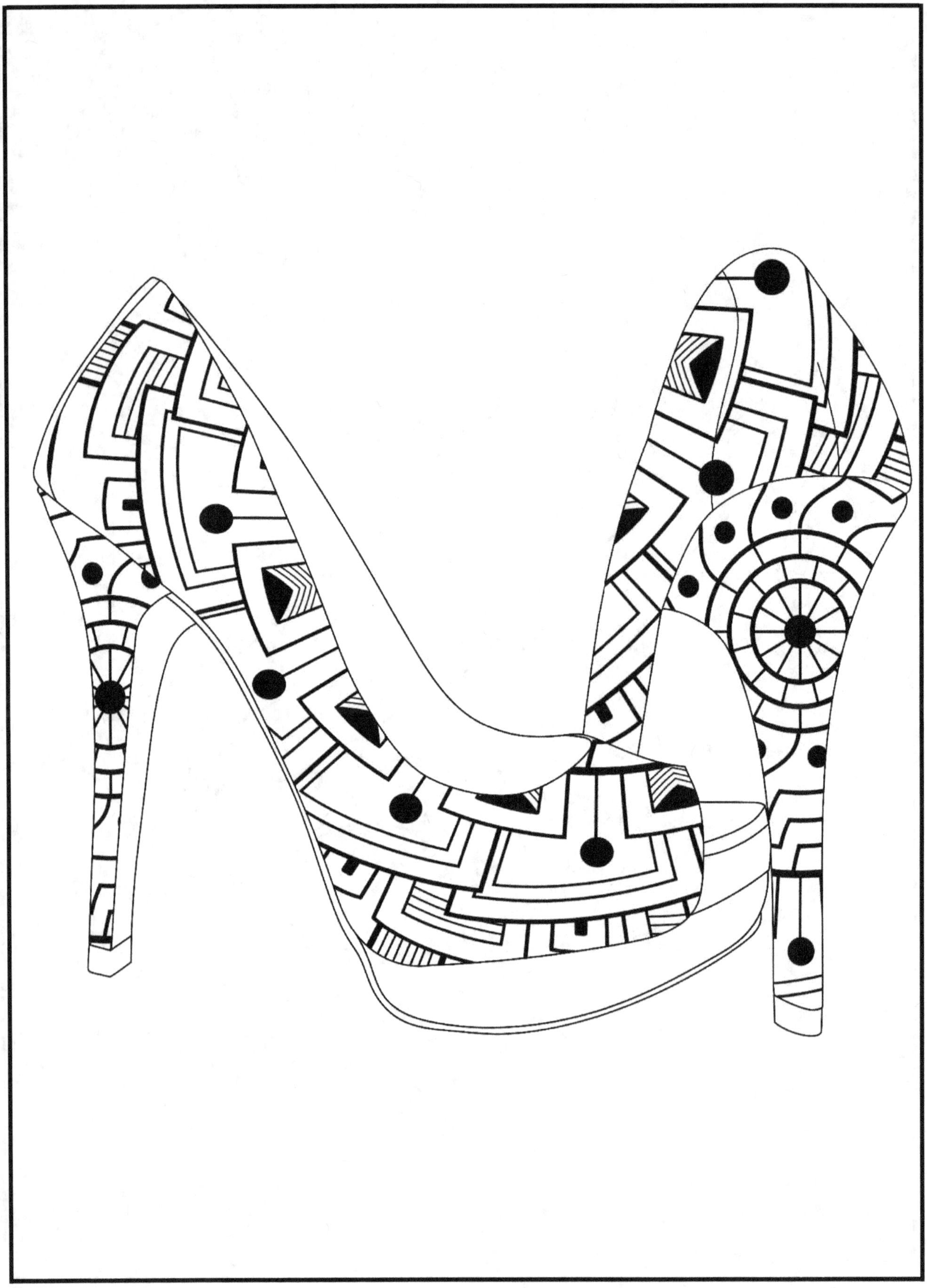

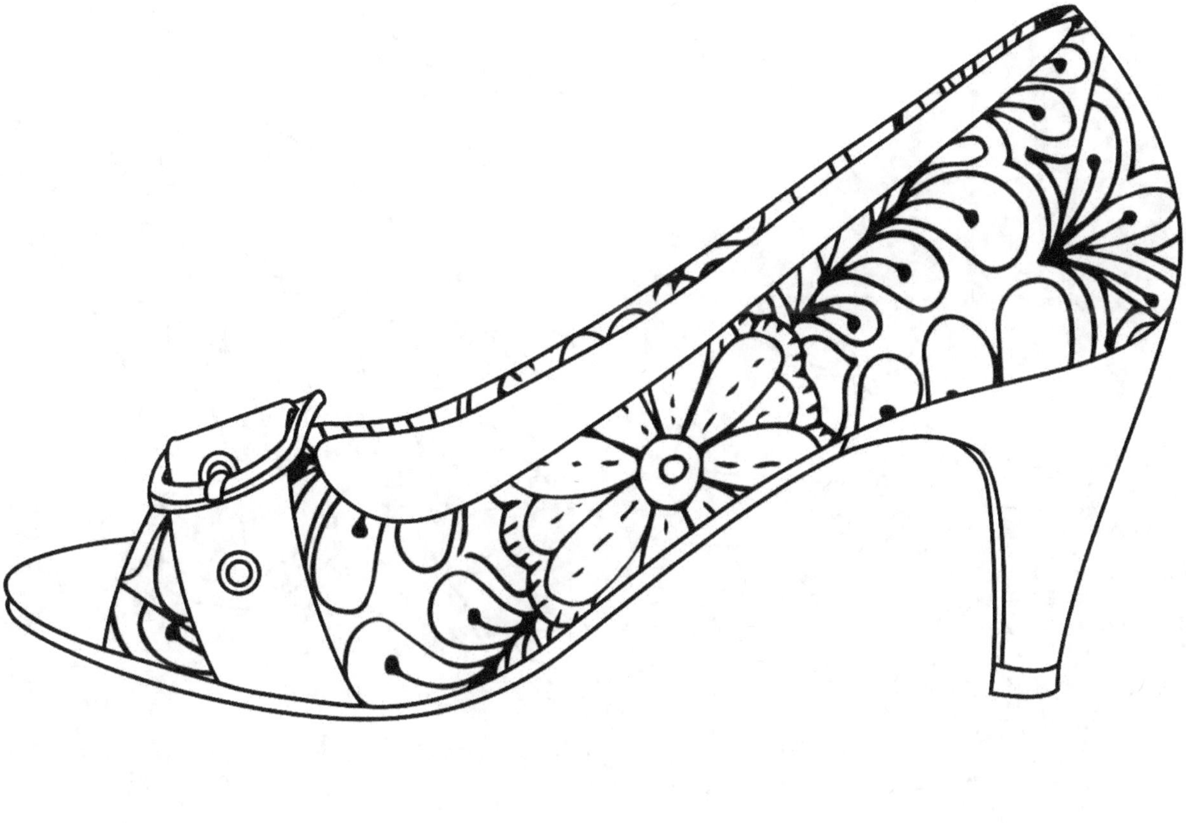

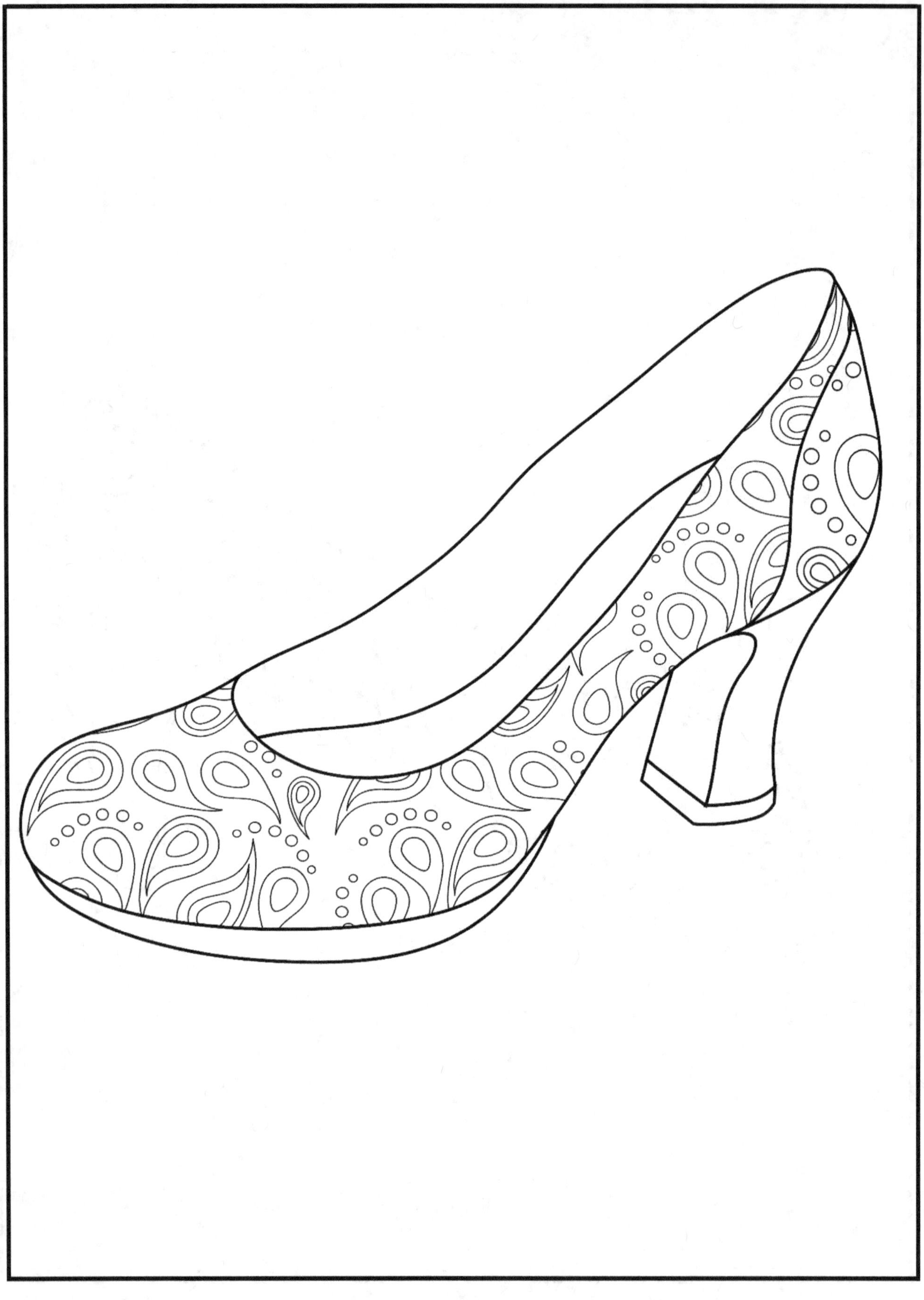

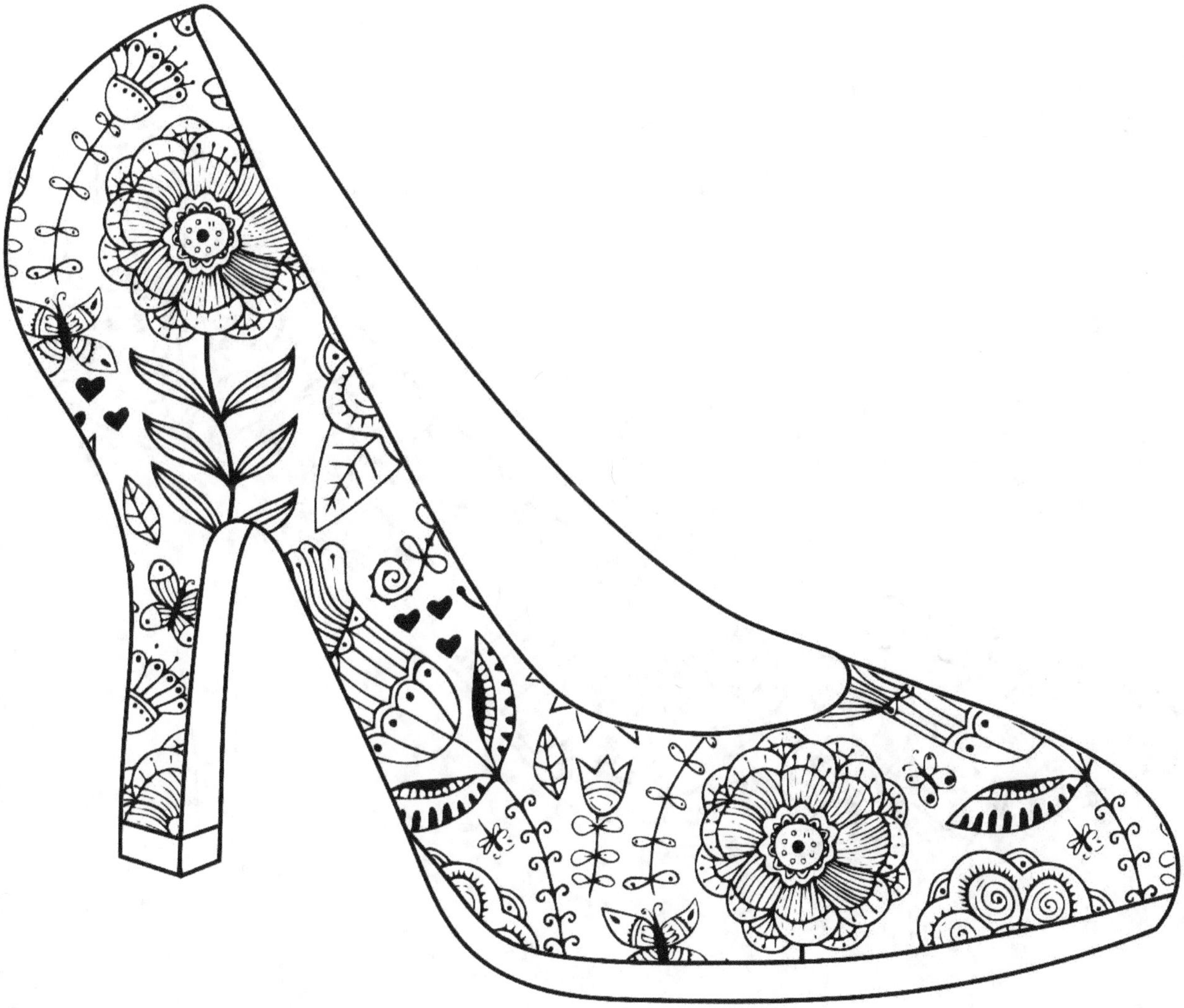

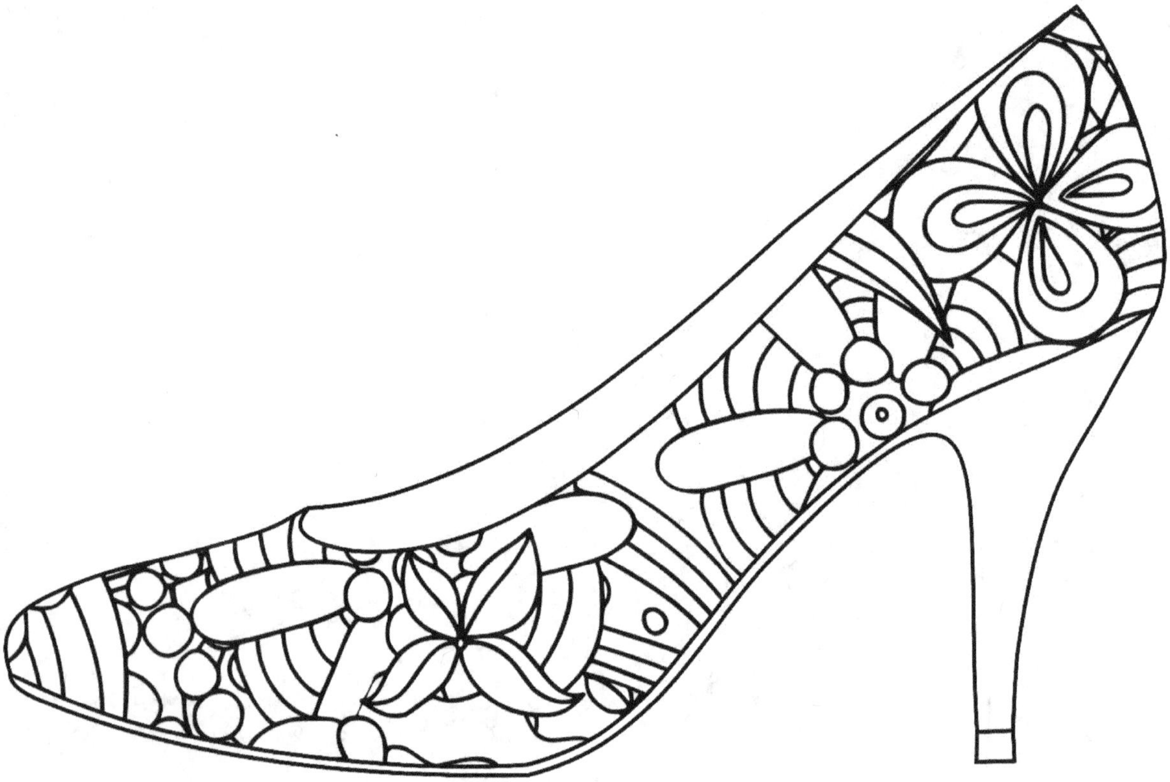

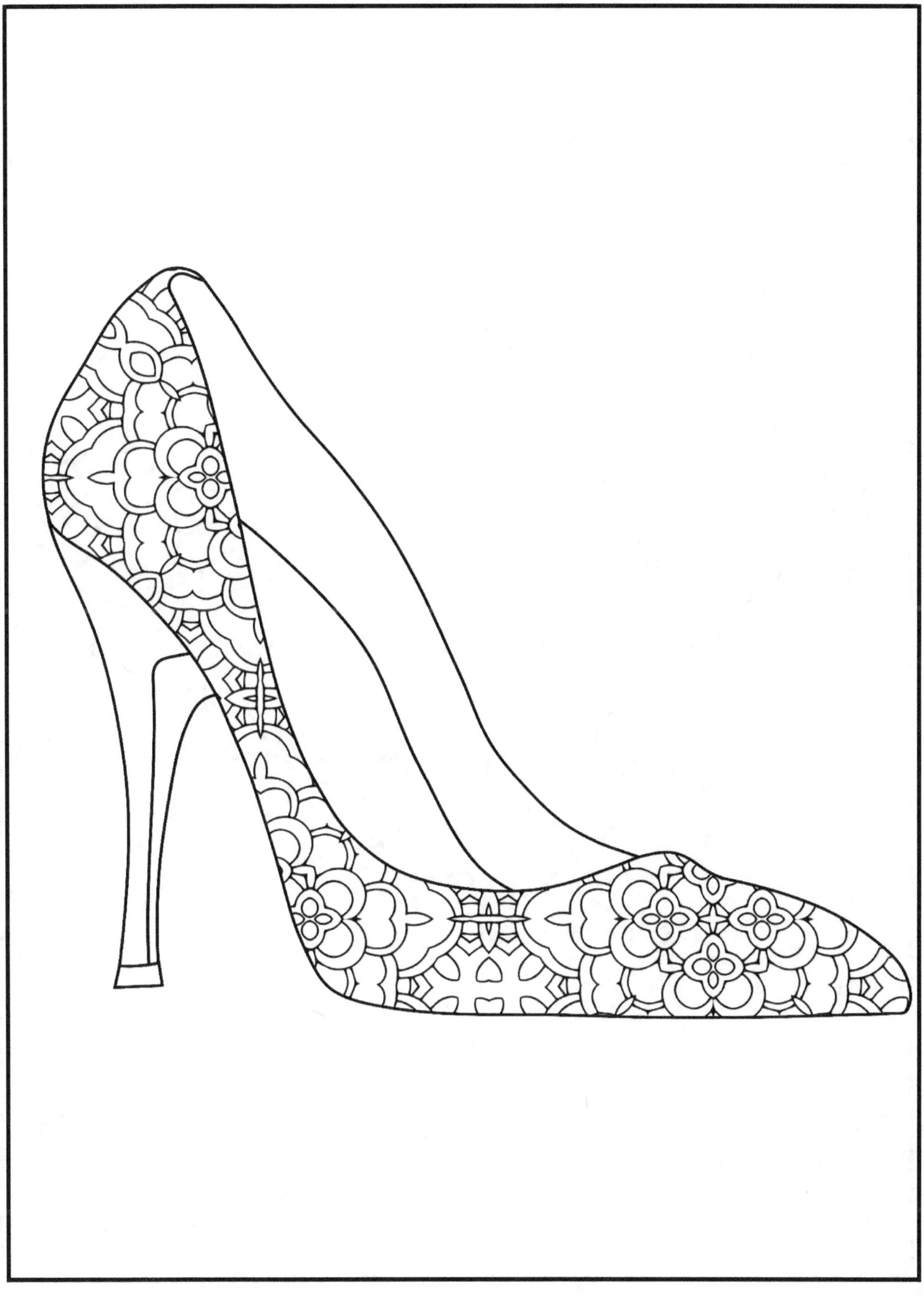

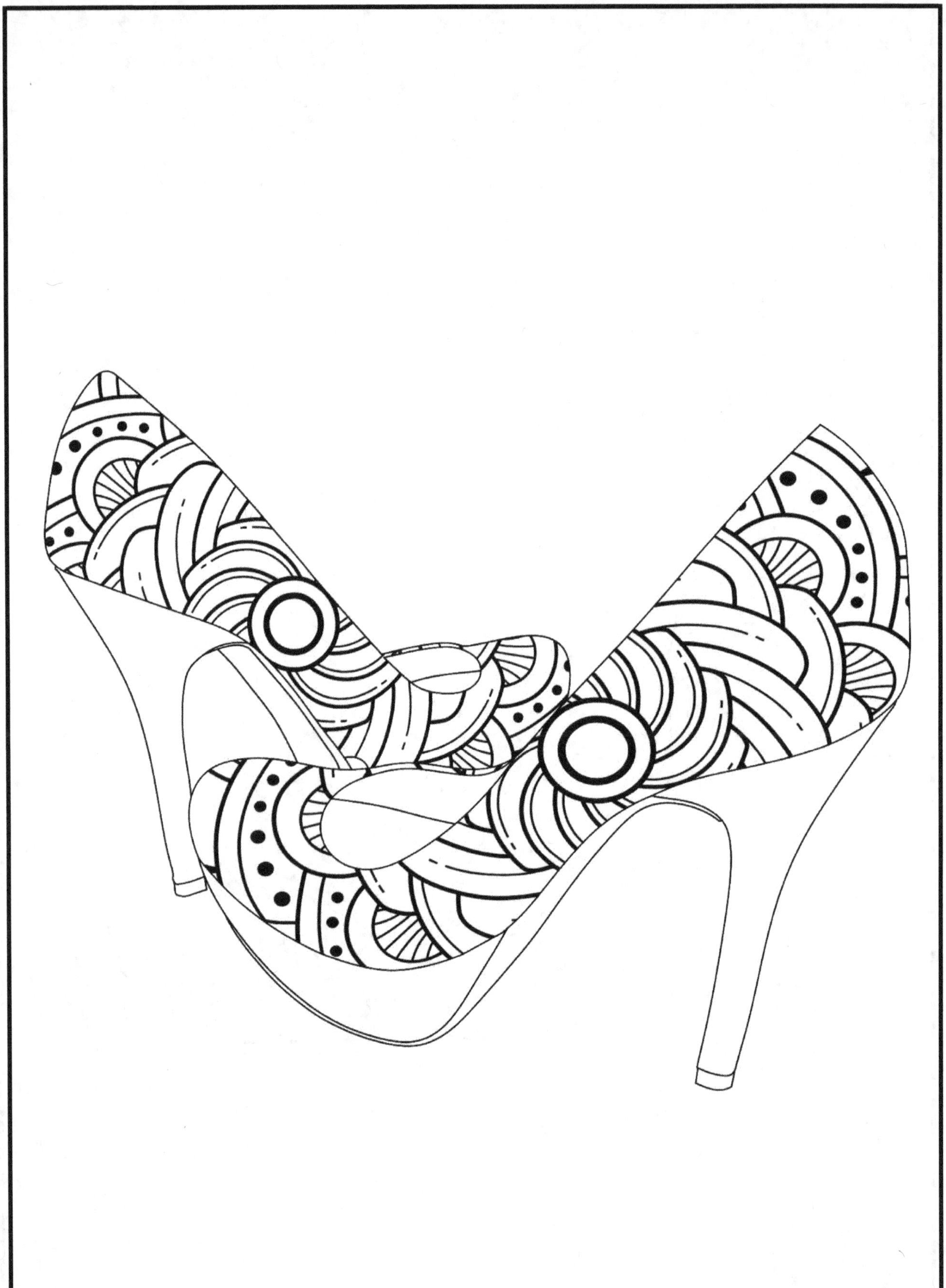

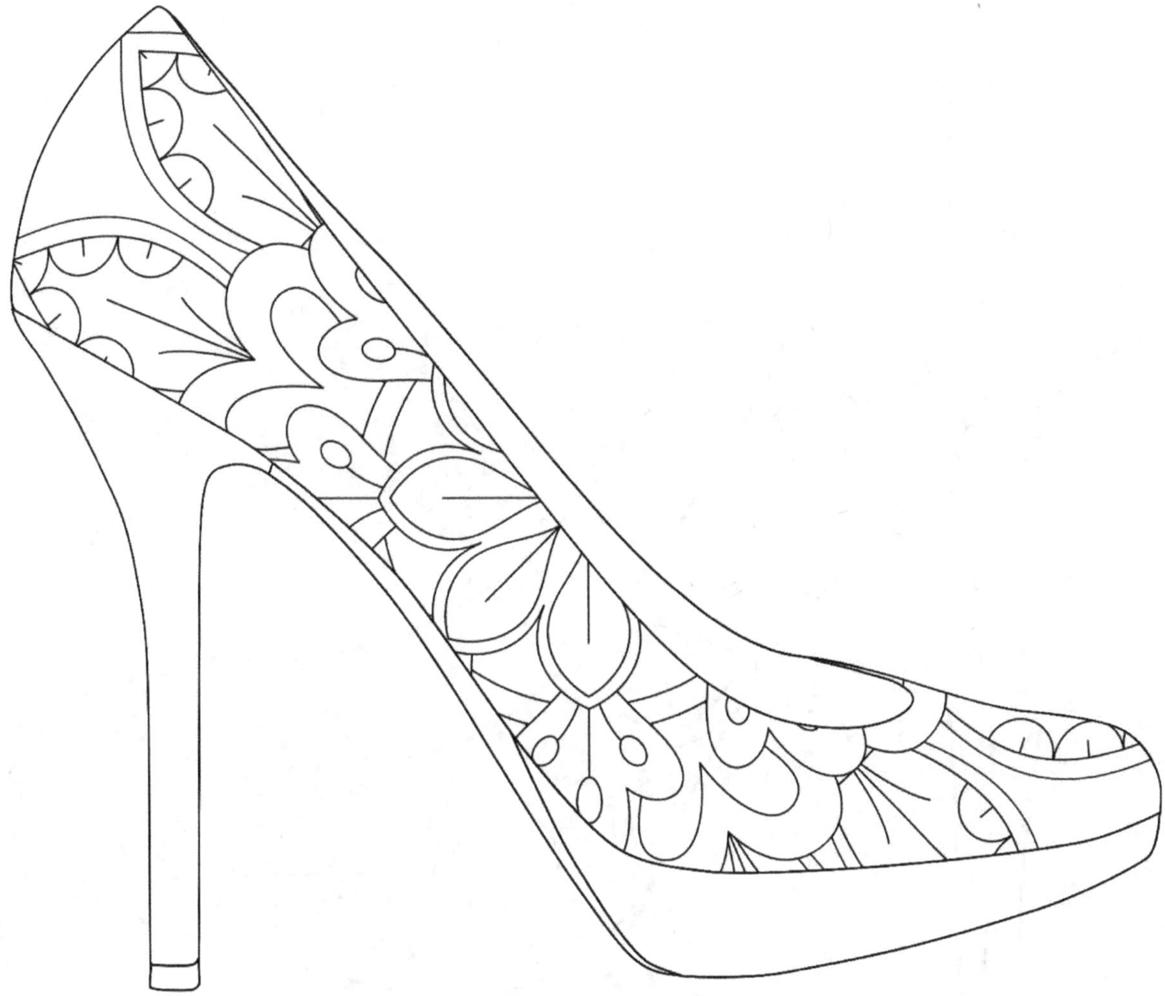

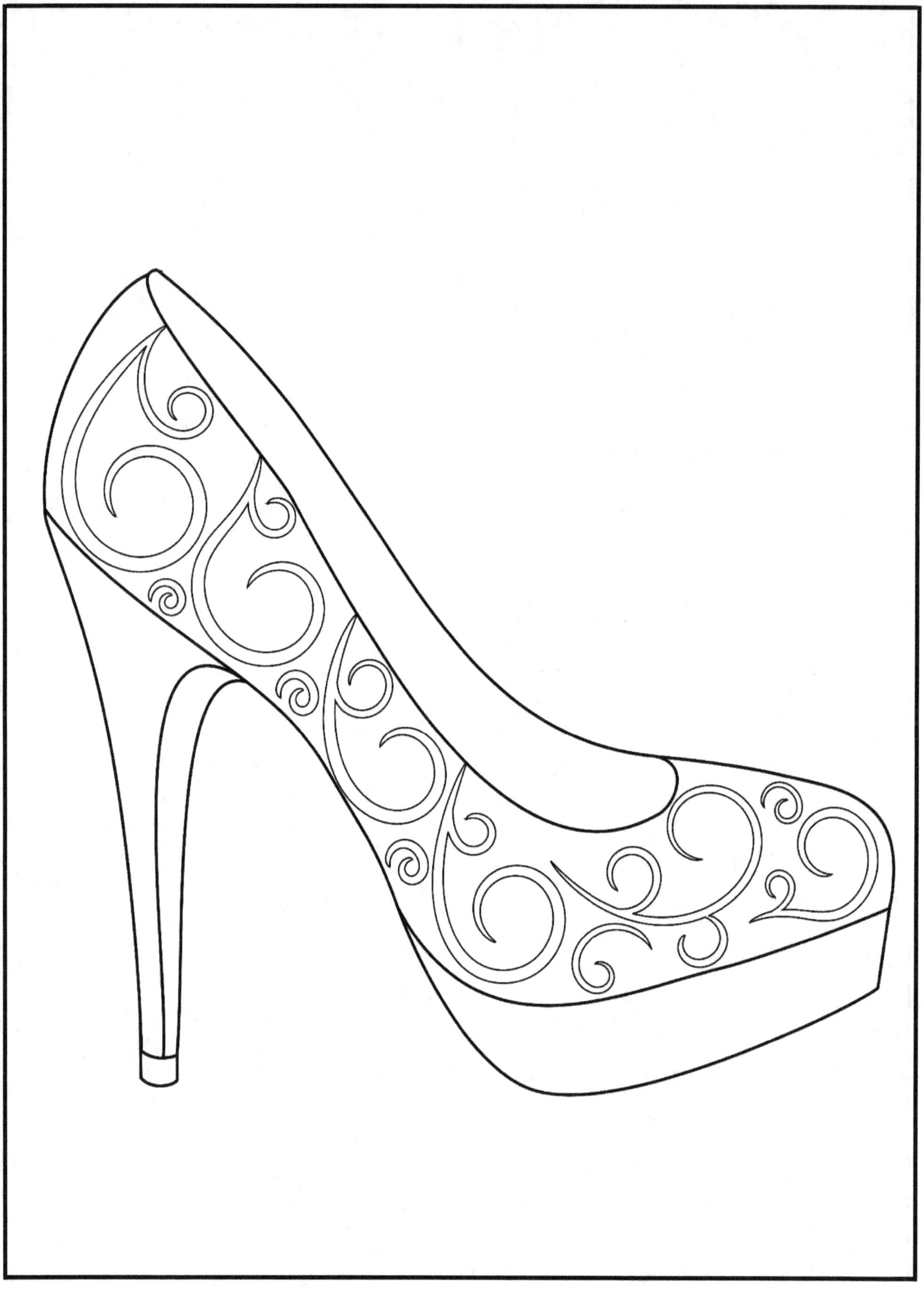

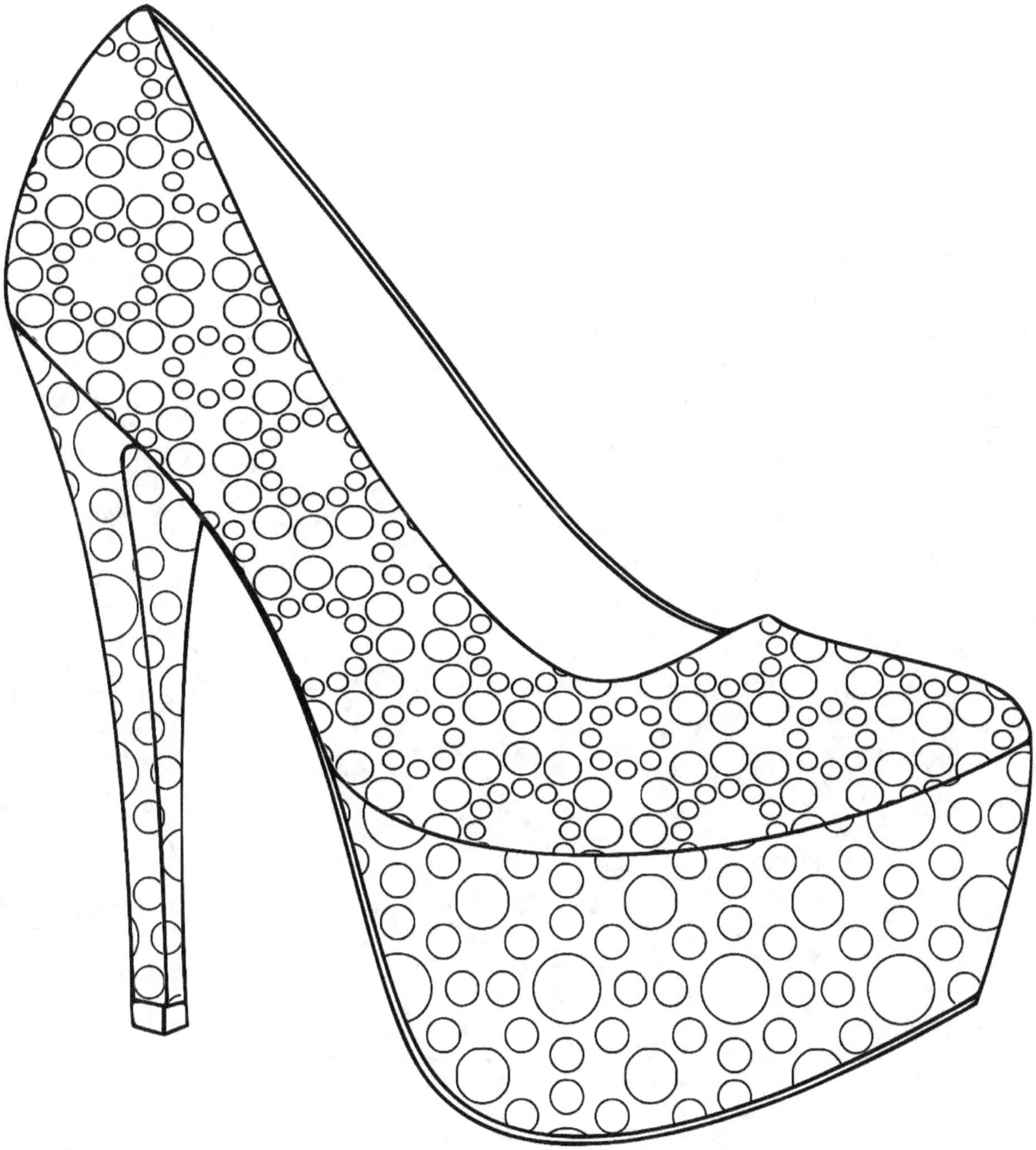

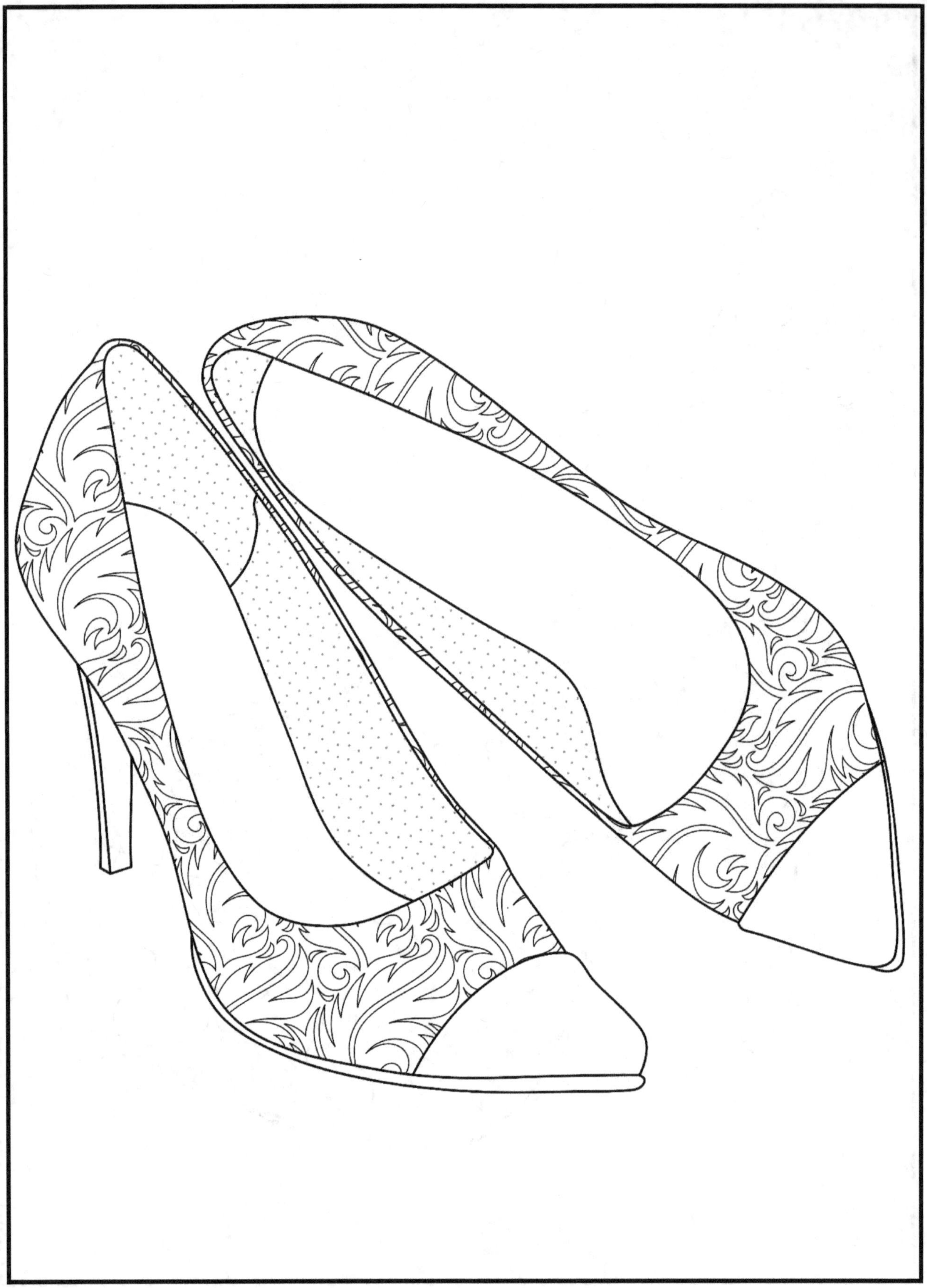

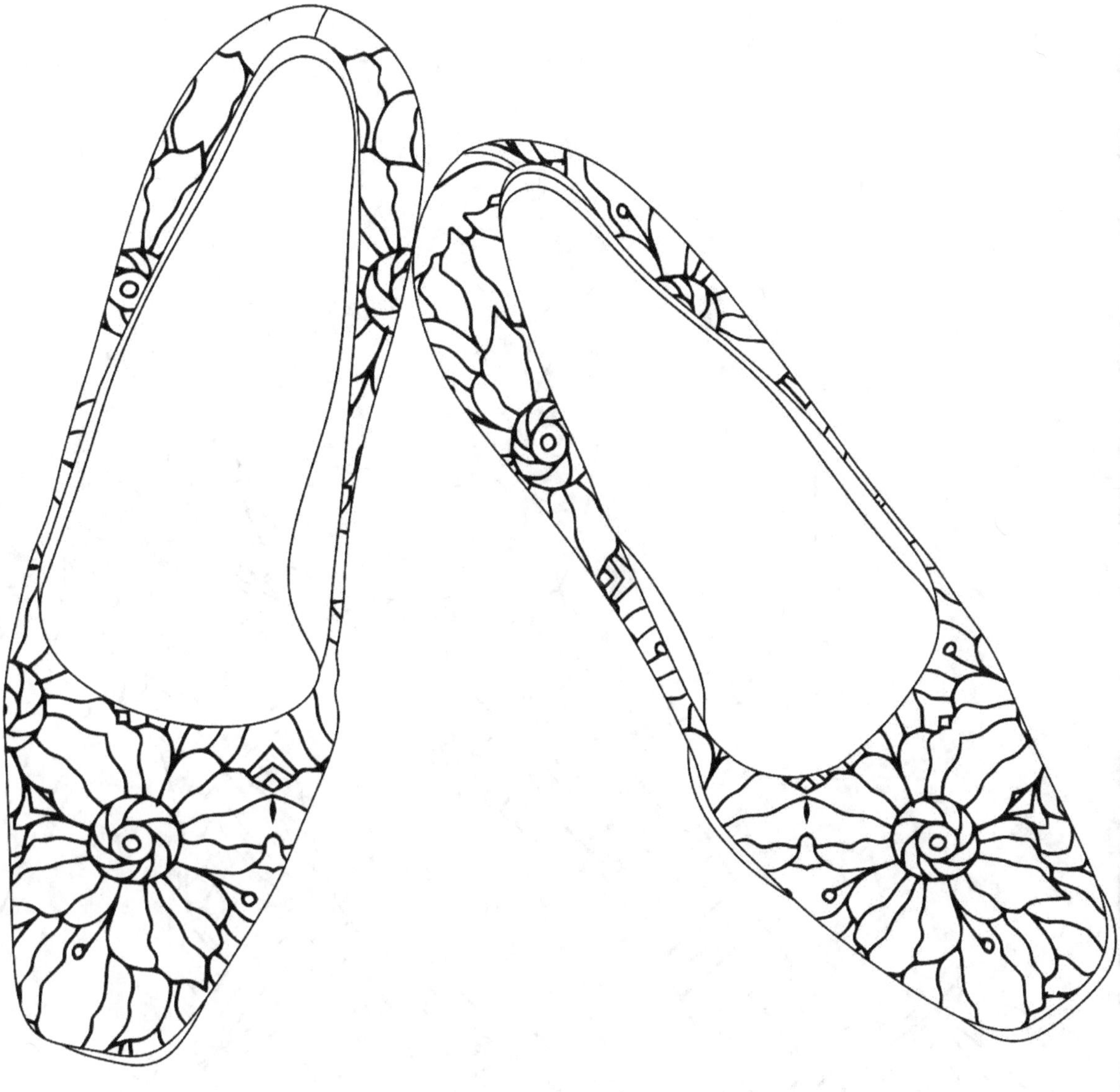

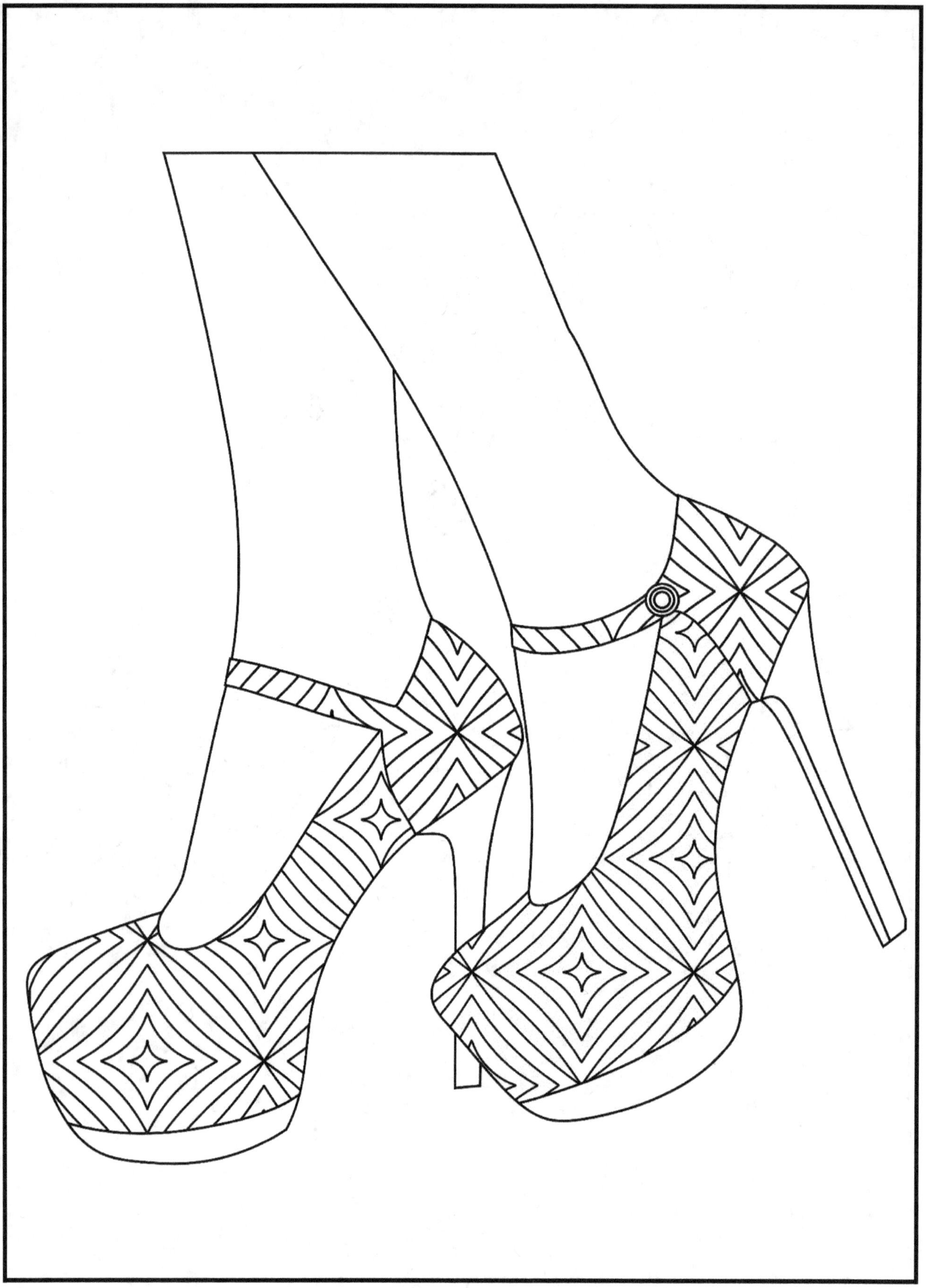

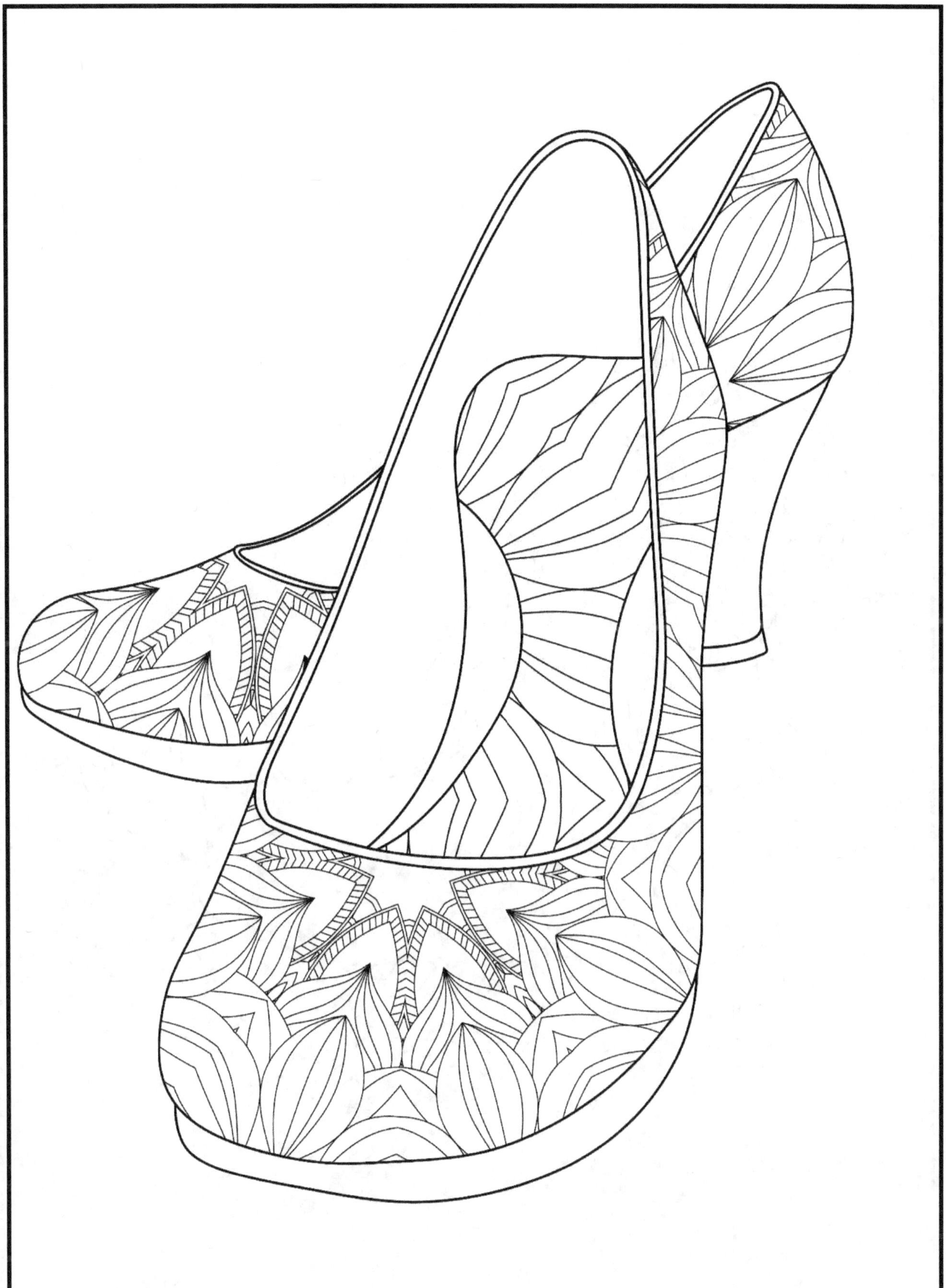

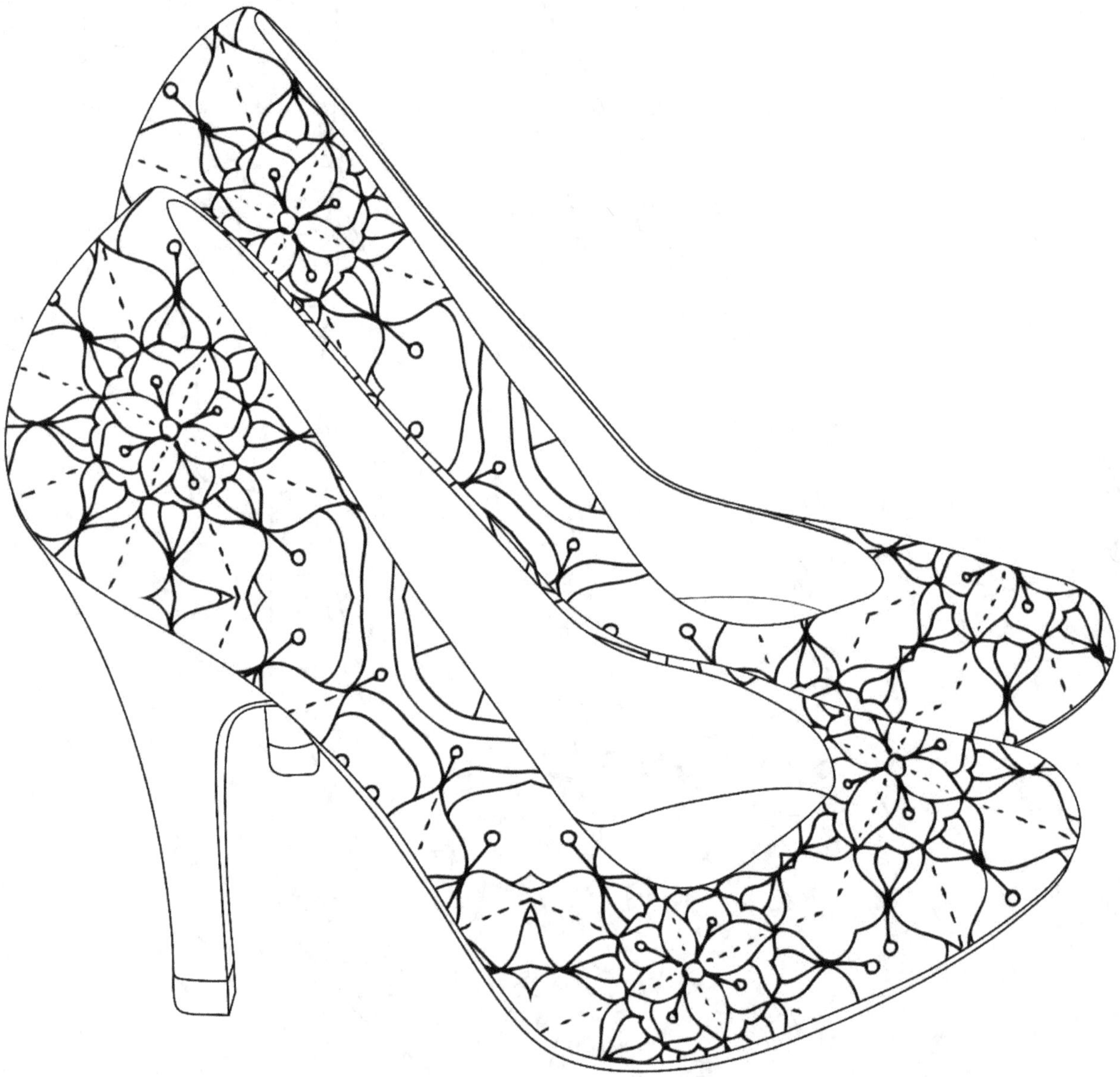

www.ingramcontent.com/pod-product-compliance
Lightning Source LLC
Chambersburg PA
CBHW080337290526
45791CB00013B/3057
* 9 7 8 1 0 7 0 5 1 7 4 8 3 *